17/2/14

EssexWorks.

- 7 FEB 2015

- 7 FEB 2015

Rely on Thomas Cook a~
travelling companion on your next tr~
and benefit from our unique heritage.

Thomas Cook **traveller** guides

CALIFORNIA
Robert Holmes

...nce 1873

Thomas Cook

Written by Robert Holmes, updated by Lisa Voormeij
Original photography by Robert Holmes, Fred Gebhart and Maxine Cass

Published by Thomas Cook Publishing
A division of Thomas Cook Tour Operations Limited
Company registration no. 3772199 England
The Thomas Cook Business Park, Unit 9, Coningsby Road,
Peterborough PE3 8SB, United Kingdom
Email: books@thomascook.com, Tel: +44 (0) 1733 416477
www.thomascookpublishing.com

Produced by Cambridge Publishing Management Limited
Burr Elm Court, Main Street, Caldecote CB23 7NU
www.cambridgepm.co.uk

ISBN: 978-1-84848-444-3

© 2004, 2007, 2009 Thomas Cook Publishing
This fourth edition © 2011
Text © Thomas Cook Publishing
Maps © Thomas Cook Publishing/PCGraphics (UK) Limited

Series Editor: Karen Beaulah
Production/DTP: Steven Collins

Printed and bound in Spain by GraphyCems

Cover photography © Corbis Nomad/Alamy

Contents

Introduction

The 'Golden State' of California is one of the best-known areas on earth, if not from personal experience then vicariously through the media and movies. Its history is remarkable. In only 150 years, it has grown from a wilderness of desert and mountains to be the world leader in high technology. It has the eighth-largest gross national product in the world, and each year it adds another 350,000 to its population.

From rugged coastline and towering redwood forests, to tranquil fertile valleys, snowy peaks and stark desert, California's geography is impressive. As the third-largest state, claiming the second-highest peak in the country and having the lowest expanse of dry land, California also doesn't hesitate to be home to two world-famous cities: Los Angeles and San Francisco.

These great cities are not all that California is assured of. Charming Victorian architecture still proudly stands in both picturesque villages and big, innovative cities. Epicurean food, wonderful wines and top-notch shopping complete the picture. Let us not forget the influential progressive politics, hundreds of outstanding museums, galleries and zoos, and historic missions and ghost towns.

To experience this state to its fullest, the car truly rules. Virtually all corners of California can be driven to along well-maintained networks of freeways, highways and country roads. However,

to most tourists, country roads in California will still resemble a motorway rather than a one-car-width lane.

Regarding activities, California has infinite opportunities. Take the

THOMAS COOK'S CALIFORNIA

California became a popular destination for travellers as soon as Thomas Cook opened up the US to British travellers. It featured in Cook's first round-the-world tour of 1872–3, and in 1876 the first dedicated tour to California was organised.

Pullman Cars made the 3,000-mile journey on the transcontinental railroad from the eastern ports to Merced. Here passengers transferred to stagecoach to visit Yosemite Valley (which had become one of the world's first National Parks in 1890). Yosemite was explored by stagecoach or on horseback. The train then continued on to San Francisco for sightseeing.

Cook's inaugural 1876 expedition included all the elements of a present-day tour – right down to tours of Napa Valley vineyards. Only Los Angeles, which began to grow in the 1880s, and Disneyland, which came much later, were not included.

challenge on the highest mountains, see ever-shifting sand dunes or kayak the jewel blue lakes. Walk along the Golden Gate Bridge at dusk and watch the famous fog lift, or spot a celebrity in Hollywood and then have brunch with Mickey Mouse.

Discover hidden fortune-cookie factories, browse through iconic bookshops or get surfing lessons in the cool Pacific.

Welcome to California and be inspired as countless artists, poets and writers have also always been.

Sea mist on the Big Sur coast

The land

In many ways California is more like a country than a state. It is big. Of the 50 united states only Alaska and Texas are bigger. The coastline stretches for 2,036km (1,265 miles) from the mist-shrouded redwood forests on the Oregon border to the hot, dry deserts of Mexico, and it is the most fertile state in the Union. Yet, in spite of its size, most of the 37 million population choose life on the geological fault line, or more accurately on a series of fault lines, extending along the whole coastal region.

California is still a landscape under construction and its situation on the junction of two tectonic plates has resulted in some of the most dramatic and contrasting scenery in North America. At 4,421m (14,505ft), Mount Whitney is the highest mountain outside Alaska and is a mere 145km (90 miles) from Bad Water, which, at 86m (282ft) below sea level, is the lowest elevation in the western hemisphere. California has three mountain ranges, three desert systems, thousands of lakes, and forests where you can find not only the tallest trees in the world but also some of the oldest and the largest.

California can conveniently be divided in two, with San Francisco as the hub for northern California and Los Angeles for the southern part of the state. The majority of visitors will fly into one of these hub cities.

The most northerly part of the state, bordering Oregon, is a wilderness of lakes and forests known as the Klamath Mountains. For the angler, hunter, birdwatcher or hiker there is enough territory to explore to last a lifetime. On the northern coast, giant redwoods have been the basis of a timber industry that has provided the main economy for the region.

Further inland, the seismic nature of the state is dramatically evidenced in the moon-like landscape of Lava Beds National Monument and the two volcanoes that are at the end of the chain that includes Mount St Helens in Washington. Mount Shasta, with its five permanent glaciers, rises to 4,316m (14,162ft) above the lake of the same name. The southernmost link in the chain is 3,189m (10,462ft) Lassen Peak, which had its last major eruption in 1915 and now forms the basis of Lassen Volcanic National Park.

On the eastern border of the state with Nevada at 1,829m (6,000ft) above sea level lies Lake Tahoe, covering an area of 518sq km (200sq miles) and surrounded by the mountains of the Sierra Nevada. Every winter, this is the centre for Olympic-class skiing at resorts such as Squaw Valley. In the summer it transforms into a hikers' paradise.

The Sierra Nevada mountains stretch 644km (400 miles) south from Tahoe. They were created ten million years ago after the oceanic plate began undercutting the continental plate to form California. Two million years ago glaciers carved out the valleys and granite domes for which the Sierra is famous. Apart from being the highest mountain range in the continental United States, it is one of the fastest growing on earth, rising at a rate of 5cm (2in) a year.

The Sierra Nevada forms the eastern boundary of the Central Valley, which is one of the most fertile and productive agricultural areas of the nation. Long, dry summers and wet winters, together with rich alluvial soil that supports everything from cotton to grapes, make the valley ideal for large-scale crop farming.

San Francisco Bay is one of the best natural ports in America and the largest natural harbour on the West Coast. Fed by 16 rivers, it covers 1,036sq km (400 square miles) and joins the sea at the 5km (3-mile)-long strait of the Golden Gate. The Bay is actually a drowned river valley – the waters are 97m (318ft) deep beneath the Golden Gate Bridge but go down to a depth of only 30m (100ft) under the eastern section of the Bay Bridge.

The coastal area from the city of San Francisco down to San Diego is the most heavily populated part of the state and boasts one of the most ethnically diverse communities in the United States.

North of San Francisco down as far as Santa Barbara in the south, Sonoma and Napa have the perfect combination of soil type and climate to produce some of the world's best wines.

Southern California is dominated by the metropolitan area of Los Angeles with a population of 14.8 million, giving it true megacity status. Urban sprawl and freeways extend from Santa Monica down as far as Newport Beach and inland to San Bernardino, an area bigger than some east-coast states. The coastal highway continues south to San Diego, California's first settlement and now its second-largest city, with a population of 1.3 million within its administrative limits. Driving on beyond San Diego you enter Mexico.

To the east of all this urban development is desert. The desert starts where the Sierra Nevada mountains and the Central Valley end and continues down into Mexico and across to Arizona and New Mexico. Three great desert systems, the Mojave, Colorado and Great Basin, combine to form part of the world's third-largest arid region. This is the land of the cactus and sage brush, sand dunes, and some of the highest-recorded temperatures on earth – in Death Valley, a shade temperature of 56.7°C (134°F) has been recorded.

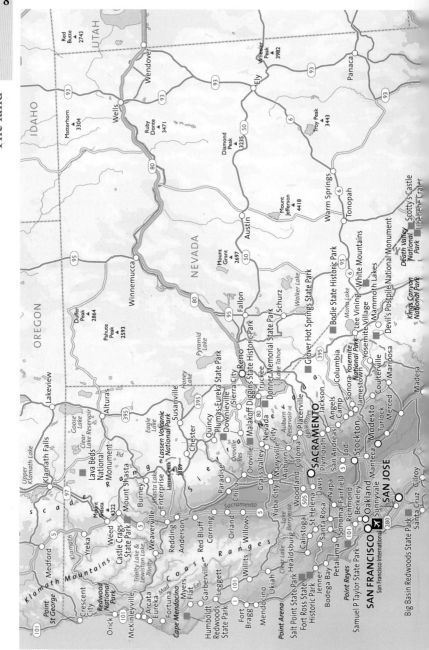

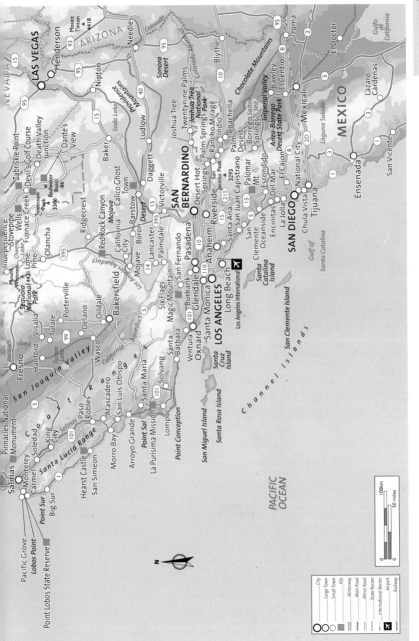

History

18,000 BC– AD 1500 Migrants from Asia cross the Bering Strait and populate the Americas. By the 16th century California is inhabited by 105 Native American tribes speaking more than 100 dialects.

1542 Juan Rodríguez Cabrillo discovers San Diego Bay while on an expedition to the north looking for gold and spices.

1579 Francis Drake, before his knighthood, reputedly lands to the north of San Francisco in the *Golden Hind* and claims the territory for England, naming it Nova Albion.

1769 Father Junípero Serra and Juan Gaspar de Portolá establish the first permanent European settlement in San Diego. El Camino Real is built along the route of present-day Highway 101.

1775 The first ship sails into San Francisco Bay. Within a year the Spanish have founded the Presidio (Fort).

1776 Mission Dolores, the first settlement of San Francisco, is established by the Franciscans. The same year Juan Bautista de Anza reaches San Francisco at the head of the Mexican overland expedition.

1781 Spanish families establish Los Angeles with 41 settlers.

1812 Russians build a trading post at Fort Ross near Bodega Bay.

1821 Mexico attains independence from Spain.

1822 California declares allegiance to the newly independent Mexico.

1826 Overland arrival of Jedediah Smith from across the Sierra Nevada signals the beginning of the US migration westward.

1846 US settlers attempt the unsuccessful 'Bear Flag Revolt'.

1848 Mexico cedes California to the US following the Mexican-American war.

	James Marshall discovers gold in the American River.	1945	The original UN Charter is signed in San Francisco.
1849	Gold Rush increases population of San Francisco to 24,000.	1955	Disneyland® opens.
		1967	Ronald Reagan is elected governor.
1850	California becomes the 31st state of the Union, with its capital at San Jose.	1984	Olympic Games held in Los Angeles.
1869	First transcontinental link established with the linking of Central Pacific and Union Pacific railroads.	1989	Worst earthquake in San Francisco since 1906.
		1992	Riots in Los Angeles.
1873	First cable cars run in San Francisco.	1994	Major earthquake disrupts Los Angeles.
		2001	Dot-com bubble bursts.
1890	Congress establishes Yosemite National Park.	2003	Arnold Schwarzenegger is elected governor.
1906	The great earthquake and fire in San Francisco. First film studio opens in LA.	2007	Wildfires destroy land around San Diego and LA.
1920	Population of Los Angeles overtakes San Francisco at 576,673.	2008	Hillary Clinton wins the Democratic primary in the state. Barack Obama wins the federal election, the first African American to become president.
1932	Olympic Games held in Los Angeles.		
1933	Dust Bowl refugees arrive from the Midwest.	2011	Jerry Brown is inaugurated as governor with one main focus: cleaning up the state budget crisis.
1937	The Bay Bridge and the Golden Gate Bridge open.		

Politics

In California, politics has become a struggle not of men but of forces. Once seen as an abundant and promised land, the Golden State in recent years has come up against severe limits. Drought, runaway growth, economic deficits, pollution and a host of other factors have combined to push the state up against the wall. Yet there remains in Californian politics a dream that fuels life here on the edge of the continent, and gives birth to the trends and tastes of America.

The main political battleground is the state capital of Sacramento. As a centre of government in the United States, Sacramento is second only to Washington, DC. It is the training ground of US congressmen, presidents and Supreme Court justices, in addition to being the home of innovative government policy.

California also plays a crucial role in national politics. The state sends more legislators to the US House of Representatives than any other. It is the biggest prize in presidential elections as well, giving the winner 55 electoral votes – 20 per cent of the total electoral votes needed to win a presidential election.

Despite California's liberal reputation, it has elected a succession of conservative Republican governors including, of course, Ronald Reagan. In recent years, the state has seen both environmental and economic problems grow to gigantic proportions. The responsibility for finding solutions to the state's many problems changed hands in 2003 when Republican Arnold Schwarzenegger became governor. He was re-elected in 2006.

Democrat Jerry Brown was elected in 2010 and became governor in 2011. With one of the highest unemployment rates in the country and a serious budget crisis, he has a challenging time ahead of him.

Welfare reform

California, like the rest of the US, faces a government deficit growing at an alarming rate. Drastic measures are being sought to bring this runaway fiscal situation under control. Naturally, debate is heated between the conservative Republicans and the more liberal Democrats.

Environmental issues

In a car culture state where freeways (motorways) were born, lumber (timber) companies rule and thirsty fertile valleys grow most of the nation's fruit and vegetables, California has its fair share of environmental pressures.

The northern part of the state is frequently in debate with the southern part regarding the usages of water, while the southern part is often questioning the northern part on their redwood trees protection acts.

Even with its 8 million vehicles in the Los Angeles Basin alone, and the close-to-extinction species of the man-made Salton Sea, this state is now leading the nation in electricity generation from renewable sources including wind, solar and geothermal power, while being one of the lowest per-capita energy-using states within the US. Current efforts to 'Save the Salton Sea' commenced in early 2011 in order to prevent further damage to this unique ecosystem. And plans for the California High-Speed Rail project are under way to help ease traffic congestion and thus vehicle emissions pollution.

Changing demographics

To walk along California's streets is to see America's ethnic future. People from every nation in the world populate its towns and cities. This rich multicultural diversity is, however, a mixed blessing. The state is seeing an exodus of people in their productive years, while more and more immigrants are children. From schools to offices, Californians are struggling to meet the needs of newcomers and keep the state's economy strong. As a visitor, however, such issues are unlikely to affect the enjoyment of your stay.

California State Capitol building, Sacramento

Culture

Of all the states in the nation, none is more culturally diverse than California. Although Francis Drake reputedly landed at Point Reyes in 1579, a few kilometres north of San Francisco, the first European settlers were the Spanish, who initially explored the southern coast and then moved up from Mexico to establish their chain of missions.

In the mid-1800s a massive influx of European immigrants made their way from the east coast of the United States in search of gold. This gave a strong European base to the population, which still exists today.

Over 37 per cent of the population is Hispanic, with the majority of these coming from neighbouring Mexico but also including Cubans, Puerto Ricans and various Central Americans. This figure does not include the thousands of illegal immigrants who continue to cross the Mexican–US border.

The massive Californian agricultural industry could not survive without this tremendous pool of labour. These immigrants (both legal and illegal), who enter the US daily, provide low-wage labour, not only for agriculture but in factories and service industries. They traditionally fill the jobs that other Californians refuse to take.

Behind this influx of immigrants is an Hispanic establishment whose families have been in California for generations. They are business owners, Congressmen and women, and leaders in politics throughout the state.

The Hispanic population tends to settle in specific neighbourhoods. East Los Angeles is 90 per cent Latino – the largest Hispanic community in the US. In San Francisco the Hispanic community is centred on the Mission District.

Every year on 5 May, the Latin-American culture throughout California explodes into festivals of song, dance and music that rival Carnival in their exuberance. This Cinco de Mayo holiday celebrates Mexican heritage and pride, attracting over 150,000 participants in San Francisco and San Jose alone.

The Asian influx started as early as 1850 when Chinese railroad workers followed the Gold Rush and started to develop their now world-famous Chinatown in San Francisco. In 1868 Japanese immigrants began to arrive at Gold Hill, El Dorado County.

In the 1970s California was a major centre for relocating Southeast Asian refugees. By 1980 there were 19 separate Asian groups in the state, the six largest being Chinese, Filipino, Japanese, Indian, Korean and Vietnamese. Between 1980 and 1990 California's Asian population almost doubled to 2.3 million people. The latest influx has also been from Southeast Asia and the newcomers are Laotians, Cambodians and Hmong. By the year 2000 Asian-Americans represented about 11 per cent of the population.

California's position as a Pacific Rim trading and banking power has helped to consolidate the state's reputation as an Asian stronghold.

Asians have made their most obvious mark through the multitude of restaurants throughout the state. Among those who have succeeded in the arts are San Francisco author Amy Tan, who won the 1989 National Book Award, and Stanford graduate David Henry Hwang, who won the Tony Award for his play *M Butterfly*.

The African-American population in California is far less significant than in many eastern states, partially due to the lack of a history of slavery on the west coast.

The only non-immigrant residents are the Native Americans, and over one million make their home in the Golden State – the largest population of any state. They have lived here for over 10,000 years.

California's rich cultural diversity is a major element in the state's charm.

Dim Sum in San Francisco's Chinatown

The diverse citizens of California

California is both the most populous state in the US and the most ethnically diverse. While 42 per cent of the state's population is Caucasian, 37 per cent are of Hispanic descent and 12 per cent are of Asian descent, with San Francisco's Chinatown being home to the largest Chinese community outside Asia – a true 'city within a city'.

These diverse demographics date back to the 19th century when the discovery of gold, silver and oil each brought an influx of migrants of many nationalities to California. The state's Hispanic heritage dates back even further with the arrival of Spanish explorers during the 17th and 18th centuries.

Native American culture, even with the highest number of Native American people and tribes, is not prevalent in California, unless the myriad casinos all over the state count. Occasional pictographs and some museums do offer an insight into early Native American culture, with the painted caves at the Lava Beds National Monument in Northern California and the relics at the State Indian Museum in Sacramento the most interesting.

Among the first Europeans to settle in California were the fur trappers from Russia and Alaska, arriving in the early 1800s. Well-preserved remnants of these explorers' dwellings are visible at the Fort Ross State Historic Park, where a Russian-style chapel from 1825 still overlooks the Pacific.

In the late 19th century, Italian fishermen arrived and settled in North Beach, San Francisco. Later, the fertile soil and warm climate tempted Italian vintners who founded what has become a highly respected wine industry in the Napa and Sonoma valleys.

The Japanese arrived in California in the 1880s to work in the fields, much like the Mexicans do today. Wars in Korea and Vietnam brought natives of these countries, along with other Southeast Asians, during the 1960s.

A Native American mural in San Diego

The political and economic troubles in Latin America and the determined promises of the Silicon Valley continued to attract immigrants, both legal and illegal, from all over the globe. Today, however, the recession and stricter immigration enforcements are two key factors in halting this trend. This will allow for an increase of California-born residents who will make up the majority of the population in the near future – a population that will hopefully hold on to its rich and unique cultural history.

San Francisco's Chinatown

Impressions

California is in many ways as familiar as our own backyards. You see it on television, you see it in films, and magazines are always featuring the latest Californian trends. Is this sun-drenched land of milk and honey all that it appears? What is the reality behind the myth?

Streets of gold

Many myths have been built on the Californian riches and lifestyle that can seem to be so alluring from the frozen climates of the north. People have been attracted to California in huge numbers since the discovery of gold in 1848. Starting from that onrush, the population has doubled every 20 years.

Spain and Mexico ruled California for almost 80 years without finding the large deposits of gold that they thought existed. Gold was finally discovered in 1848 by James Marshall just days before Mexico transferred California to the United States, which paid $18.25 million for California along with Utah, Nevada, Arizona, New Mexico and even parts of Texas and Colorado. Within ten years, 30 times that amount had been mined from the newly found mines.

California is still a relatively rich state, but the global recession of recent years has certainly had an impact. There is an increasing homeless problem in the big cities and people begging on street corners are a particularly common sight in Downtown San Francisco.

Food

In one sense California is certainly the land of plenty. The Central Valley is one of the world's most productive agricultural regions and the shelves of any supermarket will reflect the wealth of fresh produce available. An impressive range of fruit and vegetables is grown in the Valley and most of them are available year-round at inexpensive prices. Grapes are a major crop, and some of the world's finest wines are produced in the Napa and Sonoma valleys.

Inevitably a whole culinary trend has grown around this foundation and Californian cuisine has become synonymous with the finest in modern gastronomy. Even in the most modest restaurants the food will generally be good and plentiful. Service is always polite and highly efficient.

Water

For all practical purposes the state can be divided into two. Northern California and southern California are as different as chalk and cheese – geographically and politically. The rivalry between the two can be intense, and each area has its admirers who will accept no criticism of their chosen land.

The southern half of California is desert. The climate is warm and dry and the insatiable thirst of the giant metropolis of Los Angeles necessitates the diversion of water from the north. The sight of massed lawn sprinklers and gallons of water from washed cars disappearing down the drain is enough to make many northern Californians furious.

For several years water shortage has been a problem throughout California, not just in the south. Mild winters have failed to deliver the snow pack needed to provide meltwater to replenish reservoirs, and Los Angeles and the southern regions have had minimal rainfall. Restaurants generally now only provide water on request.

Fire

The threat of fire in parks is a real worry in California, especially in summer. In 2007, fires destroyed parts of Griffith Park and Catalina Island. Heed all fire warnings.

Ethnic evolution

The majority of Californians speak English, but California is the ultimate melting pot of cultures and each ethnic group has had its impact.

There is a very strong Spanish influence, as the state was originally a

Dragon head on float, Chinese New Year parade, San Francisco

A mural in the Mission district of San Francisco

London. Where else in the world could you find an archaeological dig on a site dating back to 1917?

When to go

If you are travelling with children the best months are June, July and August, although they can be very hot, especially in the south. This is also when major attractions such as Disneyland® are at their busiest. If you are looking for a quieter time, March, April, May, late September, October and November are more peaceful. Avoid American holidays, when you will be more likely to come across long tailbacks and choked highways.

province of Spanish Mexico. In agricultural areas it is sometimes impossible to find anyone who can understand English. There are towns in the Central Valley where Spanish is the first and only language.

The recent influx of Asians has already created areas in major cities where Asian languages predominate and even shop signs are in Asian scripts. San Francisco's Chinatown is a classic example, where tens of thousands of Chinese live in a totally Chinese environment. In Los Angeles, a Korean neighbourhood has sprung up in the last few years that is as Korean as areas of Seoul.

By any standards California's history is very recent. Any building over 100 years old is of significant importance, and if it is over 150 years old it is as revered as if it were the Tower of

Wetsuits required

What about the sun and sand? The beaches are not all golden and sun-drenched. This is not the state to visit for swimming in the sea. Certainly the weather can be warm, but the Pacific Ocean is definitely not. These are surfing waters and you will see plenty of blond, bronzed surfers wherever waves form, but the bronzed bodies will be well covered in black wetsuits to keep out the cold.

Plenty of good sandy beaches can be found, but it is the wild, rocky shores for which California is justifiably famous. From Big Sur up to the Oregon border the Pacific waves crash on to some of the most dramatic shoreline you will ever see. Further south, however, the beaches are geared more towards sun-worshippers.

Driving

For most visitors the first contact comes after picking up a rental car at the airport. Will the streets be full of budding Steve McQueens screeching round corners at high speed? Far from it. Driving on the right may be confusing and the freeway traffic may appear intimidating, but no one goes very fast. The majority of freeways have a maximum speed limit of 105–113km/h (65–70mph) and most people adhere to this. Generally you can drive at 8km/h (5mph) over the limit without worrying about speeding tickets, but you cannot completely guarantee it.

The most disturbing aspect of freeway travel is that people overtake on all sides. Theoretically there is a fast lane but it is not unusual to find someone in it pottering along at 64km/h (40mph). Fortunately lane discipline is very good, but remember to keep your eyes open and use your mirrors frequently.

In towns, especially near schools, the speed limit may be as low as 40km/h (25mph). In all cases, speed limits will be clearly posted. Speeding tickets are fairly expensive, so take care. Black-and-white California Highway Patrol cars operate on the freeways, and in towns and cities radar traps are frequently used. Drink-driving laws are extremely tough, so do not even take a chance.

Parking

Although, or maybe because, the car is such a major part of life in California, looking for a parking space, particularly in city centres, can be like the search for the Holy Grail.

The impressive span of the Bay Bridge, with San Francisco beyond

Street parking is generally regulated by meters, with time limits ranging from 15 minutes to 4 hours. The majority of meters allow 1 hour's parking and they almost all accept 25-cent coins. Feeding meters is prohibited, but it is a common practice nevertheless.

Always read notices attached to meters. On major streets in cities parking is often restricted at peak times; 7am to 9am and 4pm to 6pm are the most common hours, and during this period you will not only get a hefty parking ticket but also have your car towed at considerable additional expense, not to mention inconvenience, if you park illegally.

In business districts some meters will be allocated specifically for commercial vehicles. This will be clearly stated on both the meter and the kerb. Parking restrictions are indicated by kerb-side colour codes. Red means no parking at any time, day or night. White indicates a drop-off and pick-up zone, usually seen in front of hotels, restaurants and hospitals. Cars cannot be left unattended in this zone. Yellow is strictly for commercial vehicles and is normally only enforced during business hours. The hours will always be posted on the kerb. Green means you can park for a limited time (the amount will be posted). Blue indicates a disabled zone that is permanently reserved for cars displaying a special disabled placard. Certain meters displaying a wheelchair symbol are also exclusively reserved for motorists with disabilities.

All streets without meters or colour codes are available for parking unless otherwise posted, but remember to always park in the direction of the traffic as it is illegal to park in the opposite direction.

In most towns, parking is prohibited for a couple of hours one day of the

Seals and seagulls at Monterey Bay

It's carnival time!

week for street cleaning. This can be almost any time of the day or night, so make sure you read the small print on street signs.

For more details on driving see pp178–80.

Shopping

Service standards are generally high and there is a strong work ethic. Shops are open late and some never close. Most major supermarkets, where you can buy anything from light bulbs to whiskey, are open until at least 10pm and often until midnight. The 7–11 chain of convenience stores never closes at all, 365 days of the year, and they can be found in most towns. They stock a basic range of foodstuffs and also serve coffee and some fast foods.

Even the big department stores open late at least one night a week, and all but the smallest shops are open on Sundays. Sales are a way of life here, and most weeks one store or another will have one. The prices can sometimes be unbelievably low and, depending upon foreign exchange rates, there are some incredible bargains to be found. Local newspapers always carry advertisements with details. Look around; this is California, you will find what you are looking for – and a lot more besides!

Sales tax

Remember that sales tax is always added to the marked price in California. Nothing is more frustrating than waiting in a long queue at a till to find that the item you thought you had just enough money to buy has an additional 8.25 to 10.75 per cent added. The exact rate will depend on the town you are in.

Southern California

A region of astonishing contrasts where one can surf in the morning, ski in the afternoon and play golf in the evening. This is Southern California, with wild coast to the west, high mountains piercing the centre and scorching deserts continuing well beyond the southeastern borders.

First stop, Southern California's most populous city, Los Angeles.

GREATER LOS ANGELES

In LA, as everyone calls it, the car is king. The city is so large that walking is impractical, while public transport is rudimentary at best. Fortunately for the visitor, hiring a car is both simple and cheap, as long as you are 25 or over and hold a valid driving licence.

A few millimetres on a map can take hours to drive, a problem that is caused as much by traffic as by distance. The distances are indeed impressive. The size of Los Angeles is difficult to comprehend until you have tried to drive from one neighbourhood to another.

From the visitor's perspective, it is impossible to tell where LA begins or ends. Los Angeles County has a population of more than 10 million and covers an area of 10,575sq km (4,083sq miles) with 88 incorporated cities, and the continuous urban sprawl goes way beyond this.

Development stretches from Ventura County in the north to Orange County and Long Beach in the south, and from the Pacific coast across to Riverside County in the east.

This five-county area is bigger in terms of population than any state excluding California, New York and Texas and houses nearly 18 million people in 88,446sq km (34,149sq miles).

Driving at the speed limit, it takes over two hours to cross the conurbation. However, being able to travel at anything approaching the speed limit is considered a minor miracle. During rush hours there is so much traffic that even the most modest journey can take in excess of two hours. You could easily spend three weeks in LA and still not have time to do and see everything.

Los Angeles has it all – except for clean air. On rare days during the winter, Santa Ana winds blow away the smog to reveal the San Bernardino mountains forming a spectacular backdrop to the city. On days like this it really lives up to its nickname: the City of Angels.

Los Angeles has had much negative media coverage in the last few years, particularly relating to street violence. Although there are probably more problems here than in any other part of California, as one might expect for such a large city, the areas to which visitors are likely to travel are as safe as most cities of the world. Guard against pickpockets, take care of your valuables, and most problems will be avoided.

The pockets of potential violence are usually far away from the tourist sites. Not visiting Disneyland® because of gang wars in Watts is like avoiding Paris because of civil war in Italy.

Anaheim and around
Disneyland®
California's number-one tourist attraction includes eight 'theme' lands extending over 32 hectares (80 acres).

The lands are:
Adventureland – exotic regions of Asia, Africa and the South Pacific, with a fun Indiana Jones Adventure ride.
Critter Country – backwoods setting for Splash Mountain.
Fantasyland – fairy-tale kingdom, home to "it's a small world".
Frontierland – the world of the pioneers of the Old West.
Main Street USA – small-town America at the turn of the 20th century.
Mickey's Toontown – where cartoons come to life.
New Orleans Square – home of pirates, ghosts and quaint shops. Don't miss the Pirates of the Caribbean ride.
Tomorrowland – the world of the future. Space Mountain is the most popular ride here.

A full day is certainly not enough to do justice to Disneyland®. Get there

![The famous Hollywood sign on Mt Lee Perch]

The famous Hollywood sign on Mt Lee Perch

Los Angeles

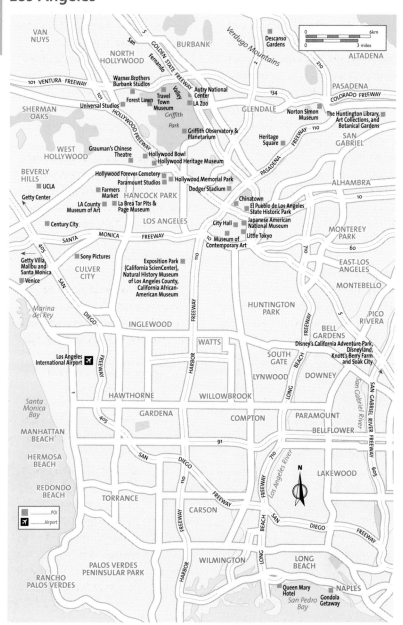

VAN NUYS

NORTH HOLLYWOOD

BURBANK

Verdugo Mountains

Descanso Gardens

ALTADENA

0   6km
0   3 miles

101 VENTURA FREEWAY

Warner Brothers Burbank Studios

GOLDEN STATE FREEWAY

San Fernando

Valley

Autry National Center

LA Zoo

134

PASADENA

COLORADO FREEWAY

SHERMAN OAKS

Universal Studios

Forest Lawn

Travel Town Museum

Griffith Park

GLENDALE

Norton Simon Museum

The Huntington Library, Art Collections, and Botanical Gardens

SAN GABRIEL

HOLLYWOOD FREEWAY

Griffith Observatory & Planetarium

Heritage Square

WEST HOLLYWOOD

Grauman's Chinese Theatre

Hollywood Bowl

Hollywood Heritage Museum

PASADENA

ALHAMBRA

BEVERLY HILLS

UCLA

Hollywood Forever Cemetery

Paramount Studios

Hollywood Memorial Park

Dodger Stadium

Chinatown

El Pueblo de Los Angeles State Historic Park

10

Getty Center

Farmers Market

HANCOCK PARK

LA County Museum of Art

La Brea Tar Pits & Page Museum

LOS ANGELES

City Hall

Japanese American National Museum

MONTEREY PARK

Century City

SANTA MONICA FREEWAY

Museum of Contemporary Art

Little Tokyo

60

Getty Villa, Malibu and Santa Monica

Venice

Sony Pictures

CULVER CITY

Exposition Park (California ScienCenter), Natural History Museum of Los Angeles County, California African-American Museum

SAN DIEGO

HUNTINGTON PARK

EAST LOS ANGELES

MONTEBELLO

PICO RIVERA

Marina del Rey

INGLEWOOD

BELL GARDENS

WATTS

Disney's California Adventure Park, Disneyland, Knott's Berry Farm and Soak City

Los Angeles International Airport

FREEWAY

SOUTH GATE

HARBOR

BEACH

LYNWOOD

DOWNEY

Santa Monica Bay

HAWTHORNE

WILLOWBROOK

San Gabriel River

MANHATTAN BEACH

405

GARDENA

COMPTON

PARAMOUNT

BELLFLOWER

SAN GABRIEL RIVER FREEWAY

HERMOSA BEACH

SAN DIEGO

91

710

LAKEWOOD

605

REDONDO BEACH

TORRANCE

CARSON

Los Angeles River

FREEWAY

SAN DIEGO

FREEWAY

POI

Airport

HARBOR

WILMINGTON

LONG

LONG BEACH

PALOS VERDES PENINSULAR PARK

RANCHO PALOS VERDES

Queen Mary Hotel

San Pedro Bay

NAPLES

Gondola Getaway

N

early and list priorities with the aid of the map and brochure given at the entrance. Disneyland® is open every day of the year, with extended hours during the summer months. Weekends during the summer are the busiest time, when over 9,000 staff are employed! There are always crowds of visitors, but queues at the attractions are generally shorter at the beginning of the week.

1313 S Disneyland Dr, Anaheim (43km/27 miles southeast of Los Angeles Civic Center). To check park hours, tel: (714) 781 4565. www.disneyland.com. Admission charge.

Disney's California Adventure® Park

This attraction adjacent to Disneyland® celebrates the state of California, from wineries to Hollywood backlots, although why anyone would want to visit a pretend backlot when a half-hour drive will take you to the real thing is a mystery. But there are some unmissable rides here, not least the Twilight Zone Tower of Terror, guaranteed to produce a few screams, and the Soarin' Over California simulated hang-glider flight. Unlike Disneyland®, alcohol is served here (the posh Vineyard Room restaurant is recommended).

To check park hours, tel: (714) 781 4565. Admission charge.

Beverly Hills

For the mere mortal, Beverly Hills is a place to ogle. This super-exclusive independent township, surrounded by Los Angeles, was originally bean fields but soon became the preferred address for Hollywood celebrities.

Elegant mansions can be glimpsed hiding behind security fences and you may even spot the occasional film star, although many of the houses are more likely to be occupied by doctors, lawyers or oil barons.

Film stars Douglas Fairbanks and Mary Pickford built their home, Pickfair, at 1143 Summit Drive, and it quickly became a hangout for the Hollywood set. After Fairbanks' death, Mary Pickford lived there in complete seclusion until her own death in 1979.

The homes of the stars can be found either with the assistance of maps on sale at many street corners or more reliably on a bus tour through the town.

A more intimate brush with Hollywood can be had at the sumptuous Beverly Hills Hotel, which was built in 1912. The hotel's legendary Polo Lounge has been, and continues to be, the setting for many a Hollywood deal. If you want to be in films, this is the place to be seen.

Apart from the shopping areas around Rodeo Drive (*see p150*) there are few footpaths in Beverly Hills and walking is frowned upon.

Expect to be questioned by the police if you get out of your Ferrari or Mercedes and they find you wandering aimlessly about.

Re-creating the Pleistocene epoch, La Brea Tar Pits, Los Angeles

La Brea Tar Pits/Page Museum

These bubbling pits of liquid tar sit incongruously next to the sleek modern architecture of the LACMA on Wilshire Boulevard.

During the Pleistocene epoch over 200 different types of creature were trapped in this primordial ooze, and their perfectly preserved skeletons are still being discovered by palaeontologists in one of the richest fossil deposits ever found.

In the adjoining Page Museum are displays of many of the discoveries from the Ice Age, including skeletons of mammoths and sabretooth cat fossils. You can also see a working palaeontology laboratory.
5801 Wilshire Blvd. Tel: (323) 934 7243. www.tarpits.org. Open: daily 9.30am–5pm. Admission charge (free on first Tue of every month).

Los Angeles County Museum of Art (LACMA)

One of the best art museums in the country, LACMA never fails to impress.

Its installations cover the history of art from pre-Columbian gold ornaments to late 20th-century paintings. The museum is in the middle of an ambitious ten-year redevelopment project, including new contemporary art facilities designed by Renzo Piano. Currently, though, the main attractions are the Ahmanson Building, housing south and southeast Asian, European and Islamic art; the Art of the Americas building, containing American and Latin American art; and the Hammer Building, housing Impressionist and post-Impressionist works. You could easily spend a whole day here – and, thanks to the museum's excellent special exhibitions, it's worth visiting repeatedly.
5905 Wilshire Blvd. Tel: (323) 857 6000. www.lacma.org. Open: Mon, Tue & Thur noon–8pm, Fri noon–9pm, Sat & Sun 11am–8pm. Closed: Wed. Admission charge (free on second Tue of every month).

Brentwood

Getty Center

Perched on a ridge in the Santa Monica mountains, a site perfectly situated to allow visitors a stunning 360-degree view of Los Angeles, the magnificent Getty Center houses a priceless collection of both fine and decorative arts.

The 45-hectare (110-acre) campus houses five pavilions: North, East, South, West and Exhibitions. The art is arranged chronologically, starting in the North (pre-1600) and ending in the West (post-1800).

The Exhibitions Pavilion houses temporary exhibits.

A number of amenities – including a café, restaurant, shop, and frequent tours and talks – make your visit both more educational and more enjoyable. This is truly one of the world's great art experiences and deserves a whole day.

1200 Getty Center Dr, off I-405. Tel: (310) 440 7300. www.getty.edu. Open: Tue–Fri & Sun 10am–5.30pm, Sat 10am–9pm. Free admission.

Knott's Berry Farm and Soak City

Although this was originally exactly what its name implies, Walter Knott started to add attractions to the farm in the 1920s. It is now California's second-biggest tourist enticement, with over 165 rides and attractions covering over 65 hectares (160 acres).

Themed areas within the park include Fiesta Village (home of the Jaguar! roller coaster), Ghost Town (featuring the not-to-be-missed GhostRider white knuckler) and The Boardwalk (where the Boomerang sends you twisting through the air – and then does it again, backwards). Kids too young to go on such rides, meanwhile, will love Camp Snoopy. Next door to Knott's Berry Farm is their waterpark Soak City, perfect – but crowded – on hot days (note that it's closed in winter).

8039 Beach Blvd, Buena Park (35km/ 22 miles southeast of Los Angeles Civic Center). Tel: (714) 220 5200. www.knotts.com. Open: daily at least 10am–6pm but longer in summer and some weekends. Admission charge.

Downtown
Chinatown

Compared with San Francisco's, LA's Chinatown is tiny. It is easily seen on

(*Cont. on p32*)

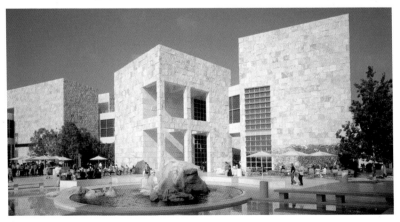

The Getty Center

The movies

Legend has it that, in 1913, when a downpour of rain greeted Cecil B DeMille in Arizona, he boarded a train and travelled west until he found sunshine. When he did, Hollywood was born.

It all started in an old barn that now houses the **Hollywood Heritage Museum** at 2100 North Highland Avenue (*tel: (323) 874 2276*). The museum is full of memorabilia from the silent movies, including a re-creation of DeMille's office.

Today most of the great studios make more films for television than for the cinema, and many of them offer tours.

In Hollywood, Paramount Studios at 5555 Melrose Avenue (*tel: (323) 956 1777*) offer a two-hour tour with a historical overview.

KCET, a Los Angeles public television station, gives technical tours of its studios at 4401 **Sunset Boulevard** (*tel: (323) 666 6500*).

Warner Brothers **Burbank Studios**, at 4000 Warner Boulevard, Burbank (*tel: (818) 972 8687*), take you behind the scenes to see the daily activities of Warner Brothers. Only small groups are accepted, but a thorough introduction to the whole process of film-making is given. The tours leave from 3400 W Riverside Drive.

An artist's view of the special effects used for the filming of the original *King Kong* in the studio

Paramount Pictures gate, Los Angeles

Sony Pictures (*10202 W Washington Blvd, Culver City*) also runs several studio tours every weekday, and you might well catch a glimpse of a show or movie being filmed. It's best to reserve in advance (*tel: (310) 244 4000; see also www.sonypicturesstudios.com*).

Of course, the granddaddy of studio tours is at **Universal Studios**, 100 Universal City Plaza, Universal City. Although this is the Hollywood version of Hollywood, it is good entertainment value, if not too authentic in other departments.

To feel a part of the scene you may want to pick up a copy of the *Hollywood Reporter*, which has covered the industry every weekday morning since 1931.

LA is also home to many tours offering glimpses of the homes of the rich and famous. These include **Starline Tours** (*tel: (323) 463 3333; www.starlinetours.com*), which offers a range of options including a two-hour bus tour of celebrities' homes (the outside, that is). A cheaper option is to buy a specialist map (vendors abound, especially in Hollywood) and do it yourself. But remember – no harassing or photographing your favourite star (should you be so lucky as to see them), as you may find yourself on the wrong side of the law!

foot and consists of the usual array of Chinese restaurants, Chinese groceries and shops selling cheap novelties imported from the Far East.

North Spring Street and North Broadway form the two main thoroughfares, with Central Plaza (947 N Broadway) the main focus. The Chinese American Museum (425 N Los Angeles St. Tel: (213) 485 8567. www.camla.org. Open: Tue–Sun 10am–3pm. Admission charge) is also worth a visit.

Exposition Park

This 65-hectare (160-acre) park close to downtown LA is the home of the 92,000-seat Los Angeles Memorial Coliseum, which was the site of both the 1932 and 1984 Olympic Games. It is also home to a farmers' market and three of the city's major museums.

California African American Museum

This museum is devoted to African-American culture and history. It is

California ScienCenter in Exposition Park, Los Angeles

housed in an airy glass building and has new exhibitions every few months. *600 State Dr. Tel: (213) 744 7432. www.caamuseum.org. Open: Tue–Sat 10am–5pm, Sun 11am–5pm. Free admission.*

California ScienCenter The museum extends through several buildings, with exhibits covering subjects as diverse as AIDS and earthquakes. This is very much a hands-on museum and most of the exhibits are interactive. The Air and Space complex is due to take delivery of retired space shuttle *Endeavour.* *Figueroa St at Exposition Blvd. Tel: (323) 724 3623; IMAX information tel: (213) 744 7400. www.californiascience center.org. Open: daily 10am–5pm. Free admission, but charge for IMAX Theater.*

Farmers' Market It is doubtful if any farmers actually make it to the market these days, but you will find a wide variety of produce stalls as well as a variety of shops. The biggest attractions are numerous snack bars and cafés serving a huge variety of foods, all at affordable prices. *6333 W 3rd St. Tel: (323) 933 9211. www.farmersmarketla.com. Open: Mon–Fri 9am–9pm, Sat 9am–8pm, Sun 10am–7pm.*

Natural History Museum of Los Angeles County At the northern end of the park lies one of the most popular museums in Los Angeles. Three floors of

galleries display everything from wildlife dioramas of America to dinosaurs and fossils, and cultural exhibits depicting life on the frontier. There's a particularly good gem and mineral gallery with a well-guarded vault devoted to precious stones and a huge gold collection. The Ralph M Parsons Discovery Center & Insect Zoo is packed with hands-on activities for children.
900 Exposition Blvd. Tel: (213) 763 3466. www.nhm.org. Open: daily 9.30am–5pm. Admission charge (free on first Tue of month).

Little Tokyo
This enclave of Japanese culture is close to City Hall. There are theatres, Buddhist temples and the Japanese Village Plaza, an outdoor shopping and dining mall.
South San Pedro St.

Japanese American National Museum
This excellent Little Tokyo museum draws out the history of Japanese immigration to the US. In addition to its permanent collection, which includes personal accounts, it also hosts temporary exhibitions.
369 E 1st St. Tel: (213) 625 0414. www.janm.org. Open: Tue, Wed & Fri–Sun 11am–5pm, Thur noon–8pm. Closed: Mon. Admission charge (free third Thur of month).

Museum of Contemporary Art (MOCA)
It may be surprising that what must surely be one of the trendiest cities on earth did not have a museum devoted to contemporary art until 1986.

It had been hoped to open the new museum in time for the 1984 Olympics, but when this was obviously not going to happen, a temporary gallery was opened that proved to be so popular that it is still in use. The Geffen Contemporary, as it is now called, is located at 152 North Central Avenue, and a free shuttle service operates between the museum and the temporary gallery.

The museum has a permanent collection of works from the major modern movements, including work by Mark Rothko, Claes Oldenburg and Cy Twombly. It also regularly features interesting temporary exhibits. The Geffen, too, holds noteworthy temporary exhibitions.

The museum as a building is worth seeing in itself: the red sandstone and glass edifice was designed by Japanese architect Arata Isozaki.
250 S Grand Ave. Tel: (213) 626 6222. www.moca.org. Open: Mon & Fri 11am–5pm, Thur 11am–8pm, Sat & Sun 11am–6pm. Closed: Tue & Wed. Admission charge (free on Thur 5–8pm).

Old Town
Close to the heart of modern Los Angeles there still remains a block of buildings dating back to the birth of the city. **El Pueblo de Los Angeles State Historic Park** preserves this historic area that was first settled in 1781. The 1818 Avila Adobe is the oldest building in Los Angeles. It is open to

the public. The other buildings line either side of Olvera Street, a pedestrianised way that is a permanent Mexican marketplace with craft shops and cafés almost obscuring the historic buildings behind. It gives a strong flavour of early Spanish California.
El Pueblo de Los Angeles Historic Park, 845 N Alameda St. Tel: (213) 485 8372. www.ci.la.ca.us. Free walking tours start at 130 Paseo de la Rosa Tue–Sat on the hour, 10am–noon.

Glendale
Forest Lawn
Cemeteries may not be a normal tourist attraction, but Forest Lawn on South Glendale Avenue, close to Griffith Park, is said to have in excess of one million visitors a year. Stars such as Clark Gable, Carole Lombard and Jean Harlow are buried here, but don't expect to be able to get close to them, or that staff will tell you their exact location.

The 121 hectares (300 acres) of lush lawns are a popular, if macabre, picnic site.
1712 S Glendale Ave, Glendale. www.forestlawn.com. Open: daily 8am–6pm. Free admission.

Griffith Park
This 1,619-hectare (4,000-acre) oasis of greenery sits astride the Hollywood Hills. It provides outdoor recreational facilities for the neighbourhood, including an 18-hole golf course and more than 85km (53 miles) of jogging, as well as hiking and bridle trails.

Park Ranger Visitor Center, 4730 Crystal Springs Dr. Tel: (323) 913 4688. www.laparks.org

Autry National Center On the northeastern edge of the park, this is an impressive museum dedicated to the 'Wild West'. Anyone with even the slightest interest in cowboys will be fascinated by the two floors of exhibits of historic artefacts and Western film memorabilia, such as the jacket worn by Robert Redford as the Sundance Kid or John Wayne's gun belt.
4700 Western Heritage Way. Tel: (323) 667 2000. www.theautry.org. Open: Tue–Fri 10am–4pm (10am–8pm Thur in summer), Sat & Sun 11am–5pm. Closed: Mon. Admission charge (free on the second Tue of every month).

Griffith Observatory and Planetarium
Although it is doubtful whether the telescopes could now penetrate more than a few metres of Los Angeles smog, the observatory is still the major landmark of Griffith Park. On a clear day the views of Hollywood and downtown Los Angeles are spectacular.

The 1930s architecture has provided the backdrop for several Hollywood films, most notably for James Dean in *Rebel Without A Cause*.
2800 E Observatory Rd. Tel: (213) 473 0800. www.griffithobservatory.org. Open: Wed–Fri noon–10pm, Sat & Sun 10am–10pm. Free admission.

Los Angeles Zoo The zoo is situated directly opposite the Autry National Center. The 46 hectares (113 acres) opened in 1966 and now house over 1,100 different animals. There is a particularly strong collection of primates and endangered species. Popular attractions include the Campo Gorilla Reserve and a new Elephants of Asia exhibit. The botanical gardens are a lovely place to wander.
5333 Zoo Dr. Tel: (323) 644 4200. www.lazoo.org. Open: daily 10am–5pm. Admission charge.

Travel Town Museum Close to the zoo, this transportation museum has a yard full of steam engines and rolling stock as well as a narrow-gauge railway on which children can ride.
5200 Zoo Dr. Tel: (323) 662 5874. www.traveltown.org. Open: Mon–Fri 10am–4pm, Sat & Sun 10am–6pm. Free admission.

Hollywood

This area was established as a religious agricultural community in 1903, only to become part of Los Angeles in 1910.

Griffith Observatory

The intersection of Hollywood and Vine has become synonymous with the glitter and glamour of Hollywood. For decades this was an exceedingly run-down area, but thanks to investment by local authorities, it is finally coming up again.

Hollywood Boulevard is the home of several legendary attractions: the Hollywood Walk of Fame, Grauman's Chinese Theatre (*see below*) and the Kodak Theatre (which hosts the annual Academy Awards ceremony).

Grauman's Chinese Theatre
Built by Sid Grauman in 1927, this cinema is one of the essential sights of Hollywood, not so much for the gaudy false Chinese architecture as for the remarkable collection of hand- and footprints of film stars such as Cary Grant, Rock Hudson, Doris Day and Joan Crawford. The extravagant interior is worth a look and guided tours are offered daily.
6925 Hollywood Blvd. Tel: (323) 463 9576. www.manntheatres.com

Hollywood Forever Cemetery
Many of the old Paramount stars are buried here. Among the palm trees and marble statues lie Rudolf Valentino, Peter Finch, Cecil B DeMille, Douglas Fairbanks and many more great Hollywood personalities.
6000 Santa Monica Blvd.
Tel: (323) 469 1181.
www.hollywoodforever.com.
Open: daily 7am–6pm.

Hollywood Universal Studios
A tour of Universal Studios is very high on the list of many first-time visitors to Los Angeles.

This is as close to 'Hollywood' as most people will ever get. It is, however, a Hollywood version of 'Tinsel Town'.

The tour takes you through the backlots covering 170 hectares (420 acres) with 36 sound stages and over 10,000 film-makers. Many of the scenes on the tour are instantly recognisable by TV and film buffs: the Psycho house, streets of façades used for any number of Westerns, even Wisteria Lane (*Desperate Housewives*) – they are all here.

Just as interesting as this behind-the-scenes experience are the special attractions, which are the most memorable. Where else is it possible to experience the full magnitude of an 8.3 earthquake while on an underground train with water mains bursting all around, and still live to tell the tale?

Aside from the tour, there's plenty to keep both adults and kids occupied for a few hours. Rides include Jurassic Park, Revenge of the Mummy, Shrek 4-D, and the new King Kong 360 3-D. When you've had your fill of excitement and need some plain old retail therapy, the adjoining CityWalk will empty your purse with its shops, restaurants and cinemas (*see www.citywalkhollywood.com*).
100 Universal City Plaza, Hollywood Freeway (101) – follow signs.

Tel: (800) 864 837. www.universalstudios hollywood.com. Open: daily – generally 10am–6pm in winter, 9am–7pm in summer, but it varies.
Admission charge.

Paramount Studios
Most of the major studios have left Hollywood for the San Fernando Valley, and Paramount Studios is the last of the greats still to occupy their lot on Melrose Avenue. Only recently have members of the public been allowed through their famous gateway, and now behind-the-scenes tours are available.
5555 Melrose Ave. Tel: (323) 956 1777. www.paramount.com. Tours: weekdays 10am, 11am, 1pm, 2pm. Admission charge, reservations essential.

Long Beach
So far from central Los Angeles that it is difficult to think of it as part of the same county, Long Beach has undergone a facelift in recent years and provides a pleasant break from the big city.

Little Italy
The neighbourhood of Naples was developed early last century and based on the canal towns of Italy. Quiet waterways are linked by a series of walkways, and what more appropriate way of sightseeing here than by gondola?
Gondola Getaway, 5437 E Ocean Blvd, Long Beach. Tel: (562) 433 9595. www.gondolagetawayinc.com

Queen Mary
The ocean liner, once the world's biggest, lies berthed in the world's largest natural harbour. The refurbished *Queen Mary* was retired to Long Beach where she opened as a hotel, museum and entertainment complex. In addition to exhibits and shows such as Ghosts & Legends, there are tours and evening events. The bar is lovely, too.
1126 Queens Hwy. Tel: (877) 342 0738. www.queenmary.com. Open: daily 10am–6pm.

Malibu
Getty Villa
The former home of J Paul Getty, the Getty Villa occupies a stunning location overlooking the ocean at Malibu. The collections of Greek, Roman and Etruscan artefacts, which are arranged thematically, are impressive, too. Note that, although entrance is free, reservations are required.
17985 Pacific Coast Hwy.
Tel: (310) 440 7300. www.getty.edu. Open: Wed–Mon 10am–5pm. Free admission.

Marina del Rey
This pleasant seaside neighbourhood lies conveniently close to both Los Angeles International Airport and downtown Los Angeles.
There is not really any sightseeing here, but overlooking the Marina del Rey harbour is Fisherman's Village. Its colourful Cape Cod-style buildings house speciality shops

and restaurants that are open daily all year round.

Pasadena

Pasadena came to prominence in the late 1900s because of its agreeable climate. Only 20 minutes by freeway from downtown Los Angeles, the town sits at the foot of the San Gabriel Mountains.

Driving around the town will give a good impression of past and present wealth, with many very fine houses on tree-lined avenues.

The historic centre of the town has been restored over the last few years and, in a ten-block area known as 'Old Town', pawn shops and adult bookshops have given way to art galleries and trendy restaurants. Fortunately the original Victorian façades are being preserved.

The Huntington Library, Art Collections, and Botanical Gardens

It would be difficult to find a more impressive collection of paintings and

Pasadena City Hall exterior

manuscripts anywhere. Of the four million items in the recently renovated and expanded Huntington Library, several are of unique value. The Ellesmere Manuscript of Chaucer's *Canterbury Tales* dates back to around 1400. There is a two-volume Gutenberg Bible printed on parchment in 1455, a Shakespeare Folio edition and Audubon's original edition of *Birds of America.*

The art collection is equally impressive, covering 18th- and 19th-century French and British Art (such as Gainsborough's *The Blue Boy*). The Huntington's gardens (stretching some 49 hectares/120 acres) are also a wonderful place to stroll; highlights include the Desert Garden and the Japanese Garden. A casual, buffet-style 'afternoon tea' is served in the Rose Garden's tea room (*at weekends, the first sitting is at 10.45am; reservations required*).
1151 Oxford Rd, San Marino. Tel: (626) 405 2100. www.huntington.org. Open: Memorial Mon, Wed–Fri noon–4.30pm, Sat & Sun 10.30am–4.30pm. Admission charge (free first Thur every month – advance ticket required).

Norton Simon Museum

This unusual modern group of buildings houses an impressive collection of art spanning 2,500 years. It includes paintings by Rembrandt, Raphael and Rubens; drawings by Goya; sculpture by Rodin and Moore; and works by Cézanne, Van Gogh and Degas.

Major collections include French art, from Poussin and Watteau through to the Impressionists and on to the Cubists, and Southeast Asian art. Several galleries are devoted to Degas, and the museum has countless models for his bronze figures.

411 W Colorado Blvd, Pasadena. Tel: (626) 449 6840. www.nortonsimon.org. Open: Mon, Wed, Thur, Sat & Sun noon–6pm, Fri noon–9pm. Closed: Tue. Admission charge (free on first Fri of every month from 6–9pm).

Santa Monica

Santa Monica is a beach town with one of the best piers in California as its focus.

Here you will find the California of the Beach Boys, bronzed surfers, body-builders working out, and every kind of performer and musician. On the beach, just by the pier, volleyball courts are in constant use.

The pier itself has a multitude of games, shops, restaurants, an early 20th-century carousel with hand-painted horses that was featured in *The Sting*, plus a roller coaster and landmark Ferris wheel.

Pedestrianised Third Street Promenade has a variety of shops and restaurants; those on Montana Avenue, to the north, are trendier.

Venice

The best way to describe Venice is trendy. Walking along the boardwalk you will be passed by just about every form of human-powered wheeled

Dinosaur topiary on Third Street Promenade, Santa Monica

transport in existence – roller skates, bicycles, monocycles, skateboards – along with the usual array of joggers and surfers.

In the summer the beach is packed with sun-worshippers and the parking problem becomes a nightmare.

At all times of year there is plenty of activity. Up near 18th Avenue is Muscle Beach where aspiring Arnold Schwarzeneggers can be watched pumping iron, while at the southern end of town is a 335m (1,100ft)-long pier. The shops and restaurants on Abbot Kinney Boulevard reflect the neighbourhood's friendly and eclectic feel.

Only three blocks away from all this activity is the small area of canals that gave Venice its name (*see p40*).

Walk: The Venice canals

This is the only area of Venice's canals that has been preserved. This quiet, residential neighbourhood provides peaceful relief from the frenetic activity of Venice Beach.

Allow 1 hour.

From Los Angeles take the Santa Monica Freeway (I-10) west to Venice Boulevard. Follow Venice Boulevard west to the ocean. South Venice Boulevard leads to a car park on the seafront. During the summer this fills very early, but there are a few other car parks in the area.

Walk back from the car park on the right-hand side of the street for three blocks until you pass over a small bridge crossing the Grand Canal. Steps lead down to a footpath that runs along the length of the canal.

1 Grand Canal

Cigarette manufacturer Abbot Kinney had a dream of creating a Venice of America. Twenty-six kilometres (16 miles) of canals were dredged from the Santa Monica Bay swamps in 1905, but the discovery of oil spelt doom. The canals became polluted and by 1929 the city had most of them filled in. This one section of the Grand Canal is all that remains.

Walk along the bank to the far end, past the back gardens of an assortment of cottages. Fortunately the snarling dogs that seem to be everywhere never materialise and remain safely behind fences. On your left you will pass four canals running at right angles to the Grand Canal.

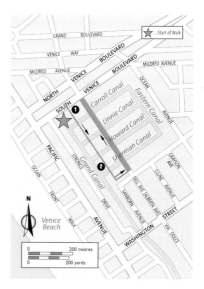

2 Sherman Canal

The houses that back on to the canals are an interesting architectural mix, varying from modest cottages to mini-palazzi. Too expensive for the far-out, bohemian fringe of Los Angeles, they attract latter-day yuppies with artistic inclinations.

The attraction of this area is obvious as you stroll along the footpaths. Where else in this giant metropolis can you find the quiet, European atmosphere provided by this early 20th-century dream? Cross the bridge over the Sherman Canal, the last of the four, and just meander back along the footpaths and enjoy this oasis of tranquillity in the heart of Los Angeles. Dell Avenue cuts through the canal area and this will take you straight back to South Venice Boulevard whenever you are ready.

If you need refreshment, Venice boardwalk has several fast-food vendors, but it's much nicer to head to Abbot Kinney Boulevard, in particular the stretch between North Venice Boulevard northwest towards Main Street. Here you'll find lots of trendy cafés, restaurants and shops. The pick of the eateries includes **Abbot's Habit** (No 1401), **3 Square Café & Bakery** (No 1121) and **Jin Patisserie** (No 1202).

Walk: The Venice canals

Houses along one of the few surviving canals in Venice, Los Angeles

Beach life

The most sought-after houses on the southern coast of California face the beach – no matter that the fog rolls in and the ocean is cold.

The beach plays a major part in the lives of Californians. From Malibu down to Laguna, whatever the weather, on any day of the week, people can be seen using this narrow strip of sand between the land and the sea.

Surfers are always searching for the perfect waves and often find them north of Malibu. Anglers use every structure that juts into the sea to cast their lines. Joggers jog and skateboarders skate.

At Santa Monica and Venice Beach, the weekend brings out a veritable circus of street performers. Jugglers, people on roller skates, weightlifters and fast-food vendors are all out in force competing with each other for the ever-present audience.

Muscle Beach in Venice is a popular place to watch the blond gods of the Pacific coast pumping iron and impressing the girls (and boys!).

The girls are no less hesitant about impressing the boys, skating along the boardwalks in the skimpiest of bikinis.

Volleyball is played in earnest wherever there is an open stretch of

Surfers at dawn near the Huntington Beach Pier, Huntington Beach

Roller-skating at Santa Monica Beach

sand. Hermosa Beach has a televised world volleyball championship during each summer.

Not all the beaches are pretty. Huntington Beach has ugly oil derricks along the coast and offshore, and this hunger for offshore oil is a frequently raised topic of considerable environmental controversy.

In the northern part of the state the beaches are more popular with rugged outdoor enthusiasts. Here, waves continually crash on to the rocky coastline and cold winds blow in from the Pacific Ocean. It may be the sunny state of California but this northern coast has a true northern climate.

SAN DIEGO

San Diego is the ideal holiday destination. The climate is superb, with warm, sunny days that the Pacific breezes prevent from getting too hot. It rarely rains (a problem for residents but not for visitors), it never freezes, and the average annual daytime temperature range is between 14°C (58°F) and 21°C (70°F). It has 113km (70 miles) of sandy beaches and plenty of attractions, including what is considered to be the world's finest zoo.

Most of the 3 million residents of San Diego County live within 48km (30 miles) of the ocean, and the sea plays a major role in everyday life. This is the headquarters of the 11th Naval District, one of the world's largest fleets of fighting ships.

There is history too. This is the birthplace of California. Father Junípero Serra established his first mission here in 1769, but over 200 years before that the Portuguese explorer Juan Rodríguez Cabrillo landed in what is now San Diego Bay and claimed it for Spain. The 'Old Town' has been made into a State Historic Park.

Just 32km (20 miles) from downtown San Diego and you are in Tijuana across the border – but remember to take your passport.

In spite of being the eighth-largest city in the United States and California's second-biggest city, with a population of over one million, there never seems to be the pressure of time that occurs in Los Angeles. The international airport must be one of the most convenient in the world, being situated only 5km (3 miles) from the heart of the city. Downtown hotels can be reached within minutes of leaving the airport.

Balboa Park and environs

See map p49 for all sights and attractions.

Botanical Building

Right in the centre of the park, behind the lily pond, is a building that looks like a huge overturned basket. In fact, the steel framework was made for a station belonging to the Santa Fe Railroad, but was purchased for the 1915 Exposition.

It now houses a collection of ferns and other tropical/subtropical plants. *Tel: (619) 236 5717. Open: daily, except Thur, 10am–4pm. Free admission.*

Rocks, surf and sand on La Jolla Beach, near San Diego

San Diego

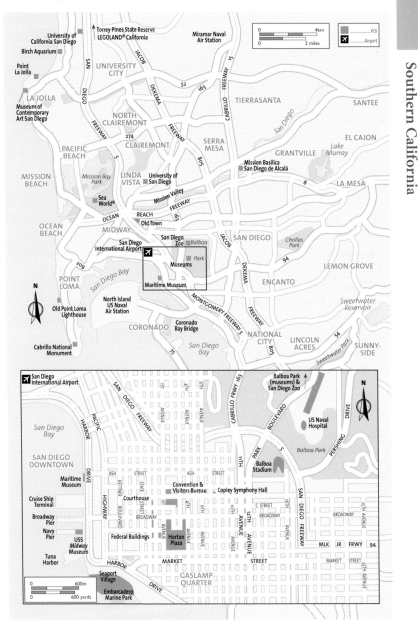

Torrey Pines State Reserve
LEGOLAND® California
University of
California San Diego
Birch Aquarium
Point
La Jolla
LA JOLLA
Museum of
Contemporary
Art San Diego
Miramar Naval
Air Station
UNIVERSITY
CITY
SAN DIEGO FREEWAY
DEKEMA FREEWAY
52
163
CABRILLO FREEWAY
15
TIERRASANTA
San Diego
SANTEE
NORTH
CLAIREMONT
274
CLAIREMONT
805
SERRA
MESA
EL CAJON
Lake
Murray
GRANTVILLE
LA MESA
8
PACIFIC
BEACH
MISSION
BEACH
Mission Bay
Park
LINDA
VISTA
University of
San Diego
Mission Basilica
San Diego de Alcalá
Sea
World®
Mission Valley
FREEWAY
163
OCEAN
BEACH
Old Town
BEACH
OCEAN
BEACH
MIDWAY
JACOB
DEKEMA FREEWAY
SAN DIEGO
Chollas
Park
LEMON GROVE
209
San Diego
Zoo
Balboa
Park
Museums
San Diego
International Airport
94
ENCANTO
Maritime Museum
POINT
LOMA
San Diego Bay
Old Point Loma
Lighthouse
North Island
US Naval
Air Station
CORONADO
Coronado
Bay Bridge
MONTGOMERY FREEWAY 5
FREEWAY
Sweetwater
Reservoir
NATIONAL
CITY
805
LINCOLN
ACRES
54
Sweetwater Park
SUNNY-
SIDE
Cabrillo National
Monument
75
San Diego
Bay
N
0   4km
0   2 miles
POI
Airport

San Diego
International Airport
SAN DIEGO FREEWAY
1ST
4TH
6TH
AVENUE
AVENUE
AVENUE
CABRILLO FRWY 163
BOULEVARD
Balboa Park
(museums) &
San Diego Zoo
N
PARK
US Naval
Hospital
PERSHING
DRIVE
San Diego
Bay
PACIFIC
HARBOR
DRIVE
Balboa Park
SAN DIEGO
DOWNTOWN
Maritime
Museum
Cruise Ship
Terminal
Broadway
Pier
Navy
Pier
USS
Midway
Museum
Tuna
Harbor
KETTNER
STATE
STREET
HIGHWAY
BOULEVARD
BROADWAY
ASH
ASH
STREET
STREET
Convention &
Visitors Bureau
Courthouse
1ST
4TH
6TH
Copley Symphony Hall
11TH
C STREET
BROADWAY
12TH
AVENUE
16TH
Balboa
Stadium
SAN DIEGO FREEWAY
BROADWAY
35TH AVENUE
Federal Buildings
Horton
Plaza
AVENUE
AVENUE
AVENUE
AVENUE
AVENUE
MLK   JR   FRWY   94
HARBOR
MARKET
STREET
MARKET
STREET
35TH AVENUE
Seaport
Village
Embarcadero
Marine Park
DRIVE
GASLAMP
QUARTER
0   600m
0   600 yards

Museum of Photographic Arts

The museum is one of the few in North America devoted just to photography. Housed in the Casa de Balboa, the gallery has regular exhibitions of prints by major photographers, and the excellent shop has a wide range of publications on photography.
Tel: (619) 238 7559. www.mopa.org.
Open: Tue–Sun 10am–5pm.
Admission charge.

Old Globe Theatre

Prestigious productions are staged at this re-creation of Shakespeare's Globe Theatre in London. It was originally built for the 1935 California-Pacific International Exhibition, burnt down in 1978 and then reconstructed, winning a Tony Award for its stage.

Also in the complex are the **Lowell Davies Festival Theatre** and the **Cassius Carter Centre Stage** (*tel: (619) 234 5623. www.theoldglobe.org*).

Reuben H Fleet Science Center

The centre houses an IMAX Dome theatre, presenting spectacular films on a hemispherical screen that envelops the audience, making them feel part of the action. State-of-the-art sound is delivered by 152 separate speakers. It also features one of the largest planetariums in the country. The Science Center is a hands-on attraction, essentially for children, covering the laws of science.
Tel: (619) 238 1233. www.rhfleet.org.
Open: daily from 10am; closing times vary from 5pm to 8pm. Admission charge.

San Diego Air & Space Museum

The whole history of aviation is covered in this circular building, from a replica of the *Spirit of St Louis* to the latest spacecraft and everything in between, including modern fighter aircraft in the centre courtyard of the museum.
2001 Pan American Plaza. Tel: (619) 234 8291. www.sandiegoairandspace.org.
Open: daily 10am–4.30pm.
Admission charge.

San Diego Automotive Museum

Situated next door to the Aerospace Museum, this museum has a display of over 80 vehicles, including horseless carriages, brass cars, performance and exotic cars, and future prototypes.
2080 Pan American Plaza.
Tel: (619) 231 2886. www.sdauto museum.org. Open: daily 10am–5pm.
Admission charge.

San Diego Museum of Art

Although this is not one of the great art museums of the world, there is a good collection that is particularly strong on Spanish Baroque and Asian art.

Adjoining the museum is a sculpture garden with a small but excellent collection by artists such as Calder, Miró, Hepworth and Moore.

As with many of the buildings in Balboa Park, the architecture is as interesting as the exhibits. The façade of the Museum of Art is a copy of the University of Salamanca in Spain.
Tel: (619) 232 7931. www.sdmart.org.

San Diego Museum of Man

Open: Tue–Sat 10am–5pm, Sun
noon–5pm, Thur 10am–9pm in summer.
Closed: Mon. Admission charge.

San Diego Museum of Man
At the core of the collection are
artefacts from the Pueblo Indians of
the southwest and the Aztec and
Mayan settlements of Latin America.

There is now a broader
anthropological base to the museum,
highlighting humankind's physical and
cultural development.
Tel: (619) 239 2001. www.museumof

man.org. Open: daily 10am–4.30pm.
Admission charge.

San Diego Natural History Museum
The environment of southern
California is the main emphasis of this
venerable institution. There are the
usual dioramas of the Californian coast
and the Fossil Mysteries exhibition.

The temporary exhibitions can also
be interesting.
Tel: (619) 232 3821. www.sdnhm.org.
Open: daily 10am–5pm.
Admission charge.

Walk: Balboa Park

Close to the centre of San Diego, Balboa Park has a higher concentration of cultural attractions than anywhere else in California. In addition to the world-famous zoo there are gardens, art venues, 15 different museums and an arts and crafts market.

Allow 1½ hours, excluding museum visits.

From downtown San Diego take I-5 north to the Pershing Drive exit and follow the signs to the zoo.

1 San Diego Zoo

A huge zoo, this deserves a day to itself. It first opened as part of the 1915 Panama-California Exposition and became one of the first zoos to put animals into a natural environment. *The walk starts by the main entrance to the zoo and follows the signs to Balboa Park. Leaving Zoo Place you will pass a miniature railway on your left.*

2 Spanish Village Art Center

Immediately on your left you will see a collection of low, Spanish-style buildings. This arts and crafts complex houses the studios of woodcarvers, potters, painters, sculptors, photographers and silversmiths, whom you can watch at work and, of course, buy the works they produce. The Center was originally built as part of the 1935–6 California-Pacific Exhibition (*open: daily 11am–4pm*). *Cross Village Place and pass between the San Diego Natural History Museum on your left and the Spanish Baroque Casa del Prado on your right. Continue to El Prado and turn left.*

3 Balboa Plaza

This is the end of El Prado. The Inez Grant Parker Memorial Rose Garden will be behind you as you look down El Prado to the landmark California Tower. You can reach the garden across the footbridge over Park Boulevard. It is an All-America Rose Selections display garden. Next to the Rose Garden is the Desert Garden with a wide variety of indigenous succulents. *Walk down El Prado between the ornate Spanish–Mexican-style buildings towards the California Tower.*

4 Lily Pond

During World War II this was used as a swimming pool for patients at the US naval hospital. The steel-frame structure behind the pond is the Botanical Building containing over 500 species of tropical and subtropical plants. *Continue down El Prado towards the*

WHERE TO EAT

SDMA Sculpture Court Café in the Museum of Art Sculpture Garden (part of the Museum of Art) serves excellent light lunches (*tel: (619) 702 6373; open: Tue–Sun 11am–3pm*).

A more interesting meal can be had at the **Prado** restaurant, set within the House of Hospitality. Even if you don't have a full meal, stop by for a sangria (*1549 El Prado; tel: (619) 557 9441; www.cohnrestaurants.com; open: lunch Mon–Fri 11.30am–3pm, Sat & Sun 11am–3pm, dinner Tue–Sun 5pm–till late*).

California Tower. Cross the Plaza de Panama, and on your left on the corner, after joining El Prado, is the San Diego Art Institute. Walk along the porticoes adjoining it and in a courtyard to the side is the Alcazar Garden.

5 Alcazar Garden

Designed for the Panama-California Exposition, 1915, it is modelled on the gardens of the Alcázar in Seville, Spain.
Return to the Plaza de Panama and turn right.

6 Japanese Friendship Garden

On your left is a traditional Japanese garden adapted to the climate and topography of San Diego. Next to the garden is the Spreckels Organ Pavilion, but unless you are in the park on a Sunday at 2pm, the world's biggest organ will be behind a metal curtain.
Return to the Plaza de Panama, turn right and retrace your path to the zoo.

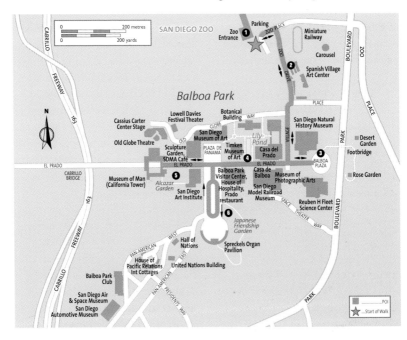

San Diego Zoo

This is often considered to be the world's greatest zoo, and for very good reasons, too.

In a time when zoos are falling both out of favour and out of business, San Diego Zoo is a remarkable success. For one thing it is big and covers 52 hectares (128 acres). There is a lot of space for the animals, and there are a lot of animals – 3,900 from 800 species, with everything from anteaters to zebras. An effort has been made to concentrate on endangered species and to develop breeding programmes for these animals.

The site of the zoo extends across a steep canyon, and to tour the zoo on foot involves some serious walking. This is certainly the best way to make the most of the exhibits, but for those unable to cope with the steep gradients there is a 5km (3-mile) double-decker-bus tour through the zoo which also provides an informative commentary. Yet another aspect of the zoo can be found by taking a trip on the Skyfari aerial tram for a bird's-eye view above the treetops.

Among the most popular habitats are the monkey and gorilla exhibits in the Lost Forest zone and the Giant Panda Research Station (with a viewing area) in the Panda Canyon zone. Add to this a children's zoo, sea lion shows, feeding sessions and special events, including walks, talks, customised tours and festivals, and you can see why many people spend a whole day here.
2920 Zoo Dr. Tel: (619) 234 3153. www.sandiegozoo.org. Open: winter daily 9am–5pm, summer daily 9am–9pm; last entry 1hr before closing. Admission charge.

SAN DIEGO ZOO SAFARI PARK

Some 56km (35 miles) to the north of San Diego off I-15, the San Diego Zoo Safari Park re-creates both Asian and African habitats on its 728-hectare (1,800-acre) site. Some 3,500 animals roam free as they are viewed from elevated walkways or on a 60-minute tour on the Wgasa Bush Line monorail. Self-guided walks are available, while Photo Caravan Safari trucks let you get closer to the animals. The Roar & Snore sleepovers are hugely popular.
15500 San Pasqual Valley Road, Escondido. Tel: (760) 747 8702. www.sandiegozoo.org. Open: daily 9am–5pm (longer hours during Festival of Lights in Dec). Admission charge.

Spanish Village Art Center

Leaving the zoo and entering the Prado area of Balboa Park you will pass a group of low, Spanish-style buildings where craftspeople and artists are busy at work turning out a variety of souvenirs for visitors.

This is very much a commercial venture, but occasionally interesting work can be found here.
Tel: (619) 233 9050. www.spanish villageart.com. Open: daily 11am–4pm.

Coronado

The exclusive community of Coronado is almost an island. A long, narrow sandbar known as the Silver Strand connects it to the mainland. Until 1969

Pair of klipspringers atop rocks, San Diego Zoo

Thomas Edison personally supervised the installation of electricity in the hotel, which at the time was the only building outside New York to be fully served with electricity.

Twelve American presidents have stayed here, and in 1977 it was made a National Historic Landmark. It was featured in the 1959 film *Some Like It Hot* and the management make great play of this, but even without the Hollywood connection the hotel is worth a visit. Wander around the beautifully kept grounds and down to the beach.

Gaslamp Quarter

In the 1800s this was San Diego's main street area but by the turn of the 20th century had become a flourishing red-light district. It is in the heart of modern San Diego and, like many inner-city areas, suffered a long period of neglect.

A concerted effort has been made to restore the district to its original glory and it has been designated a National Historic District. Many of the buildings have now been renovated. The area has still not been able to shake off its somewhat seedy image, but now the pawn shops rub shoulders with trendy new restaurants and antique shops.

There are several very fine examples of Victorian architecture, and the Gaslamp Quarter Foundation within William Heath Davis House at 410 Island Avenue can provide a free, detailed map of the district with

the only access was by ferry or a very long drive, but then the San Diego–Coronado Bay Bridge was built, and now it only takes a few minutes to drive there from downtown San Diego.

Coronado has the ambience of a different era. Although it is now only minutes from the busy centre of San Diego, it is like being in a quaint village. The affluence of the community is reflected in the immaculate tree-lined avenues and expensive houses, but, pleasant as it must be to live here, there is not a lot for the visitor to do. The main attraction is the Hotel del Coronado. This is one of the great hotels of the world, built of wood in 1888 and still in use as a luxury hotel.

histories of the individual buildings. They also offer tours on Saturdays at 11am.

Broadway to Harbor Dr between 4th & 6th Aves.
Gaslamp Quarter Foundation:
Tel: (619) 233 4692.
www.gaslampquarter.org.
Admission charge.

Horton Plaza

This colourful, modern shopping plaza, which opened in 1985, is the centrepiece for the new downtown area of San Diego. It is a textbook example of good design. The human scale and visually stimulating architecture combine with first-rate shops to make shopping here a totally satisfying experience. Even if you hate shopping it is still worth walking through the plaza just for the pleasure of the building. The car park, however, can be confusing.

On the upper level of the plaza is a wide range of restaurants and cafés serving food from all over the world and in every price range. You will also find here a seven-screen cinema and two performing arts theatres.

Between Broadway and G St, and 1st & 4th Aves.

La Jolla

Residents of this ritzy community of San Diego like to think of their neighbourhood as a separate entity and refer to it as 'The Village'. Even the post office stamps mail La Jolla although it is part of the city of San Diego. La Jolla

(pronounced 'La Hoya') is not unlike an exclusive Mediterranean resort, with the same mix of expensive houses, exquisite boutiques, gourmet restaurants and grand hotels. The cliff-lined coast adds to this impression.

It is the perfect place to walk – the intimate scale makes driving difficult. The pink **La Valencia Hotel**, a popular retreat for the Hollywood set, is the landmark building in town.

Birch Aquarium at Scripps

The best beaches in town stretch north of La Jolla up to the Scripps Institution of Oceanography, which is part of the University of California.

The aquarium here displays the marine life of the Pacific, both in tanks and in an onshore tidepool, together with displays of the latest advances in oceanography. The Tropical Seas Gallery is especially popular.

2300 Expedition Way. Tel: (858) 534 3474. www.aquarium.ucsd.edu. Open: daily 9am–5pm. Admission charge.

Museum of Contemporary Art San Diego

This prestigious museum overlooking the ocean holds a 4,000-strong collection that's particularly strong on minimalism, Pop Art, installations and works by Californian artists. The temporary exhibitions gain lots of attention, too. There are also two Downtown annexes.

700 Prospect St. Tel: (858) 454 3541. www.mcasd.org. Open: Thur–Tue

The dramatic exterior of Horton Plaza, San Diego

11am–5pm. Closed: Wed. Admission charge (free third Thur of every month, 5–7pm).

Torrey Pines State Reserve

North of La Jolla, this 708-hectare (1,750-acre) reserve and beach is one of only two places in the world where the rare Torrey pine grows naturally. The visitors' centre has hiking trail maps and runs guided walks at weekends. *Hwy 101. Tel: (858) 755 2063. www.torreypine.org. Open: daily 8am–sunset. Fee for parking only.*

LEGOLAND® California

Situated in Carlsbad, a 45-minute drive north of San Diego, LEGOLAND® is aimed primarily at children aged 2 to 12. The park itself is beautiful, while the 50-plus rides include such watery delights as Pirate Shores (expect to get very wet on Splash Battle) and Fun Tower Fire Academy. There's LEGO too, of course, in the form of Miniland USA (check out Las Vegas!). *1 Legoland Dr, Carlsbad. Tel: (760) 918 5346. www.legoland.com. Open: daily in summer, Thur–Mon in winter. Always at least 10am–5pm, and 10am–8pm for most of the summer. Admission charge.*

Maritime Museum of San Diego

This rather grandiose name is given to a flotilla of ships moored on the Embarcadero.

The highlight is the *Star of India*; built in 1863, it's the oldest iron-hulled ship in America that is still afloat. Also here is the San Francisco Bay steam-powered ferry, *Berkeley,* which played a major role in evacuating victims of the 1906 earthquake, and a 1904 steam yacht, the *Medea*, which still makes occasional trips around San Diego Bay.

1492 N Harbor Dr. Tel: (619) 234 9153. www.sdmaritime.org. Open: daily 9am–8pm, until 9pm in summer. Admission charge.

Mission Bay Park

If it can be done on water, it can be done in Mission Bay. This city-owned aquatic park is the biggest of its kind in the world.

Each watersport has its own designated area. There are six public swimming areas, which are off-limits to boats. Waterskiers have their own 2.5km (1½-mile) straight course, and jet-skiers also have their own special area free from boat traffic.

At most of the bay's marinas you can buy, rent or charter almost anything that floats, from a kayak to a skiing speedboat. Sailing and windsurfing lessons are also available at reasonable rates.

Landlubbers can rent bicycles for leisurely rides along the many bike trails over the 1,862 hectares (4,600 acres), and there are over 32km (20 miles) of running paths for joggers and walkers. For the less active there are plenty of

MARITIME MATTERS

San Diego has always had close ties with the sea. During World War II, the Korean War and the Vietnam War the city was home to the Pacific Fleet. It is very much a 'navy town' and by 1986 it had the largest concentration of naval power in the western world. There were 110,000 uniformed personnel stationed there, about 20 per cent of the entire US Navy. The 'Top Gun' attack fighter school is here too, at NAS Miramar. Every weekend, as a reminder of its presence in San Diego, the Navy docks a vessel at the Broadway Pier for the public to visit. In recent years, San Diego has been associated with the America's Cup, the oldest trophy in international sport. In 1987, the San Diego-based *Stars and Stripes* won the cup back from Australia. America's Cup memorabilia is on display at Dennis Conner Sports (*2525 Shelter Island Dr; tel: (619) 523 5131*).

fish to be caught, and tackle can be rented by the day.

SeaWorld®

This is the marine equivalent of Disneyland®, a fantasy land inhabited by all forms of marine life. This 55-hectare (135-acre) park features six major shows that are alternately staged throughout the day.

SeaWorld® really deserves a whole day to do it justice, but if time is limited there is one show that must not be missed.

The number one attraction is without doubt Shamu, a killer whale born in the park, which stars in *Believe*.

Other performing animals take part in such shows as Blue Horizons, and the new Cirque de la Mer is also impressive. But you won't get bored between shows: there are plenty of rides and roller coasters, as well as up-close (and more educational) exhibits such as Penguin Encounter, Shark Encounter and Wild Arctic, home to several of the endangered creatures. A word of warning: be prepared to get very wet!

500 SeaWorld Dr, San Diego. Tel: (800) 257 4268. www.seaworld.com. Open: daily 10am–5pm, but often later (9am–11pm on summer weekends). Admission charge.

Mission Valley

Considering the historic importance of Father Junípero Serra's first mission in California, **Mission Basilica San Diego de Alcalá** is in a curiously suburban setting. The mission is really the only site of interest in the valley and is refreshingly uncommercial.

The original mission was built in 1769 but was moved a few years later because of disputes between the Spanish and the Indians. The second mission was burnt down by the Indians in 1775 and the present mission was constructed in 1777.

Star of India, Maritime Museum of San Diego

The Spanish Mission Basilica San Diego de Alcalá, San Diego

Destroyed by an earthquake in 1803, all that remains now is a church with a bell tower and a small museum set in beautiful gardens.
10818 San Diego Mission Rd. Tel: (619) 281 8449. www.missionsandiego.com. Open: daily 9am–4.45pm. Admission charge.

Old Town

Old Town is where San Diego began; it was the first of the European settlements in California.

The State of California bought six blocks of historic buildings in the 1960s and established the **Old Town State Historic Park** in 1967. The core of the park is a traditional Mexican plaza around which many of the old buildings are located. Altogether there are 16 historic structures, plus speciality shops and restaurants.

A self-guided walking tour brochure is available free of charge at the Visitor Center in the **Robinson Rose House**, or regular guided tours are available from the Visitor Center.
Old Town San Diego State Historic Park, San Diego Ave, at Twiggs St. Tel: (619) 220 5422. www.parks.ca.gov. Museums open: daily 10am–5pm. Free admission.

Point Loma

A drive out to the **Cabrillo National Monument** at Point Loma is worth it if only for the view. On a clear day there is a sweeping view from La Jolla all the way to Mexico.

During the winter this is the ideal place to watch hundreds of California grey whales on their annual migration south from Alaska to their breeding grounds off the coast of Baja California in Mexico.

The restored **Old Point Loma Lighthouse** is a short walk away and open for visits. For hikers, there are plenty of trails down to the shore of the peninsula. One of San Diego's oldest cultural events, the annual Cabrillo Festival, is held at the park during each September.

To reach Point Loma from San Diego take Rosencrans Street to Catalina Boulevard and then follow Cabrillo Memorial Drive until you arrive at the monument.
1800 Cabrillo Memorial Dr. Tel: (619) 557 5450. www.nps.gov

Seaport Village

This modern shopping and dining complex, only a few minutes' walk from downtown San Diego, is intended to depict the harbourside as it was a century ago. It is difficult to believe that it could have been so well manicured back then, but there's no doubt it provides a very agreeable environment for shopping, with pleasant landscaped walks overlooking the harbour.

Some 6 hectares (14 acres) have been developed, with over 50 shops and 17 restaurants.
849 W Harbor Dr. Tel: (619) 235 4014. www.seaportvillage.com

USS *Midway* Museum

This decommissioned aircraft carrier museum has aircraft displays and interactive exhibits about the history of the US military. The self-guided audio tour, parts of which are narrated by *Midway* veterans, takes visitors to the captain's cabin, mess room, flag centre and other areas.
910 N Harbor Dr. Tel: (619) 544 9600. www.midway.org. Open: daily 10am–5pm. Admission charge.

Seaport Village in San Diego

THE DESERTS

No visitor to California should leave without at least one visit to the desert. In the southern part of the state the desert is all around you and within a couple of hours' drive from almost anywhere you can be in the middle of an arid wilderness. Much of the desert is a flat, barren, dusty landscape with little to commend it to the visitor. However, there are large areas of great beauty and interest that have been designated as national or state parks.

The best time to visit the deserts is between late autumn and mid-May, when temperatures are at their most comfortable level. Summer can be sizzling, but because the air is so dry it is rarely totally unbearable and the evenings are always cool and sometimes cold. Remember it is always a good idea to take water with you, even when driving on main roads, in case of a breakdown. You may well need it in the heat, and in many places traffic is infrequent at best.

Anza-Borrego Desert State Park

This is one of the largest state parks in the continental US. Over 2,590sq km (1,000sq miles) of badlands and mountains extend from the Colorado Desert to the great Sonoran Desert across the border in Mexico.

The desert was first crossed by Spanish explorer Juan Bautista de Anza in 1774 and he was commemorated by having his name added to Borrego, Spanish for the bighorn sheep now only found in the more remote corners of the park.

This is not a place for fast sightseeing. There are over 965km (600 miles) of roads, mostly unpaved, and as many footpaths. The best way to experience Anza-Borrego is to explore on foot. Nature walks are led by rangers from the visitor centre during weekends and holidays in season.

The variety of desert plants is the highlight of the park and there are several walks that show a good cross section in a short distance. Particularly notable are the California fan palms, ocotillos, smoke trees and the elephant tree, which is unique to Anza-Borrego in North America.

If you have the energy to climb some of the steeper trails, you will be rewarded with magnificent displays of several species of cactus.

Anza-Borrego Desert State Park landscape from Font's Point at sunset

Anza-Borrego Desert State Park Visitor Center

For a good view of the badlands drive up to Font's Point north of Borrego Palm Canyon.

By car, Anza-Borrego is one-and-a-half hours south of Palm Springs and two hours east of San Diego.

Visitor Center

Five kilometres (3 miles) west of Borrego Springs, at Borrego Palm Canyon, the visitor centre and museum (*closed Mon–Fri in winter*) sit buried in the desert. The building is partially underground, covered with cement and 2m (6ft) of sand. Outside the museum is a comprehensive cactus garden. *Anza-Borrego Desert SP, PO Box 299, Borrego Springs, California 92004. Tel: (760) 767 5311. www.parks.ca.gov. Open: dawn until dusk.*

Death Valley

In spite of its forbidding name, very few people have actually died here.

It was Christmas Day 1849 when the first white man gazed down at Death Valley. What has become known as the Death Valley Party consisted of four families and a group of young men. They were en route from Salt Lake City and looking for an easy way across the Sierra Nevada to the newly discovered goldfields in the San Joaquin Valley.

Twenty-six wagons went into Death Valley but only one made it out. One person died and it is said that the valley was given its name when one of the party looked back as they were leaving and said, 'Goodbye, death valley'.

Today Death Valley is a national park with over 805km (500 miles) of well-maintained roads and nearly all the attractions only a short walk away.

Death Valley is unique among desert valleys, not only because of its size and variety of scenery but also because of its extremes.

It has the lowest point in North America at 86m (282ft) below sea level, but Telescope Peak rises to over 3,353m (11,000ft) not far away. Only 123km (76 miles) to the west is Mount

Whitney, at 4,421m (14,505ft) the highest peak in the continental US outside Alaska.

In 1913 a record high air temperature of 56.7°C (134°F) was recorded and summer temperatures regularly exceed 49°C (120°F), making it undoubtedly one of the hottest places on earth.

Artist's Drive

Just south of Furnace Creek a paved road branches off into the Black Mountains. Artist's Drive, as it is called, makes a 16km (9-mile) loop through some of the most barren but colourful landscape in the world. Minerals have leached out of the ground and created a breathtaking display of colour splashed across the mountainsides. The highlight of the drive is the Artist's Palette where some fantastic colours are visible and best seen during the evening as the light of the setting sun intensifies the hues.

Badwater

The lowest point in North America is only a short walk down from Highway 178. A pond of saline water permanently occupies this depression even in the hottest months, and in the early morning you can see the reflection of Telescope Peak to the west. There are extensive salt flats just beyond Badwater. Walking out on to them is like entering a crystalline world of dazzling white stretching for as far as the eye can see.

Borax Museum

In Furnace Creek there is an outdoor museum (*tel: (760) 786 2345*) dedicated

Badwater, Death Valley, where a ground temperature of 74°C (165°F) has been recorded

DESERT WILDLIFE

To the casual visitor the desert regions may appear barren and empty, but as many as 75 species of mammal make their home here. Two-thirds of these are rodents that have most successfully adapted to the desert habitat. Larger mammals include the kit fox, the coyote and bighorn sheep.

The temperature extremes experienced in the desert regions have forced most mammals to become nocturnal, and the best chance of sighting an animal is at dawn or dusk or in the light of car headlamps.

Reptiles are more commonly seen. Several species of lizard are found throughout the region, along with five species of rattlesnake and the sidewinder (although snakes are by no means a common sight).

In spring the deserts are alive with birds – the cheeky roadrunner, of all desert wildlife, symbolises nature's ability to conquer hostile environments.

to the mineral that made fortunes in Death Valley. There is a collection of old stagecoaches, wagons and mining equipment. The oldest house in Death Valley is here, built in 1883.

Three kilometres (2 miles) north is the Harmony Borax Works, the ruins of the valley's first borax plant. An original 20-mule-team rig, looking as sturdy as it must have done in 1907, stands in front of the ruin.

Dante's View

Forty-three kilometres (27 miles) from Furnace Creek and 1,670m (5,475ft) high, Dante's View gives a 360-degree bird's-eye panorama of Death Valley National Monument. Badwater lies one vertical mile below as you gaze out across the desolate landscape. If you are up here in the early morning or late evening, take along a sweater. The temperature can be 10°C (18°F) cooler than in the valley. You might want to look out for tarantulas. In the autumn these big, hairy but generally harmless spiders are out in their hundreds looking for mates, and you can usually see them crossing the road up to Dante's View.

Devil's Golf Course

A dirt road off Highway 190 a few kilometres north of Badwater takes you to strange salt towers and brine pools. The salt here is up to 1.5m (5ft) thick and almost as pure as table salt.

Furnace Creek

Nearby springs have enabled Furnace Creek to become not only the geographical but also the commercial centre of Death Valley. Not that there is much here: two hotels, two campsites, a couple of restaurants and shops and a very large caravan site, which in the winter is full of retired people escaping to the sun.

There is also the **Death Valley National Park Visitor Center**, which has a small museum and information centre and also runs guided tours and has leaflets on self-guided tours. During the summer this air-conditioned retreat can be a very welcome relief.
*Tel: (760) 786 3200. www.nps.gov/deva.
Open: daily 8am–5pm throughout
the year.*

Scotty's Castle

By far the single biggest visitor attraction in Death Valley is both man-made and totally incongruous. At the far northern end of the valley, just off Highway 267 close to Ubehebe Crater, a flamboyant rogue and sometime prospector, nicknamed Death Valley Scotty, persuaded Chicago millionaire Albert Johnson to build an extravagant Spanish-style mansion in the desert. Scotty had originally lured Johnson out here with bogus tales of a gold mine. Johnson, however, found that the climate suited his fragile health, forgave Scotty and the two became lifelong friends.

The 25-room house has a 15m (50ft)-high living room, a music room with a 1,600-pipe organ, and even indoor waterfalls that acted as air-conditioners in the summer. Tours (50 minutes) – the only way to see inside the main house – are held daily.
Tel: (760) 786 3200. Tours: daily 9.30am–4pm. Admission charge.

Stovepipe Wells

Although this is the valley's only other town after Furnace Creek, it consists of nothing more than a store, motel, restaurant and petrol station.

However, 10km (6 miles) down the road is a remarkable area of sand dunes. Dawn is the best time to walk into them, when the footprints of the previous day's visitors have been blown away and the low dawn light casts long shadows over the sand.

Ubehebe Crater

At the northern end of the park a volcanic explosion 3,000 years ago created this huge crater 1km (1/2 mile) across and up to 237m (770ft) deep. A short walk from the car park takes you to the high point on the crater rim, with dramatic views of Death Valley against the Black Mountains.

Zabriskie Point

Take Highway 190 for 6km (4 miles) east of Furnace Creek and turn off to the Zabriskie Point lookout for one of the best panoramic views of the southern half of Death Valley.

Early-morning and late-afternoon light is particularly beautiful, and if you have time the best walk in the valley goes from Zabriskie Point down through the badlands, across the foot of Manly Beacon and on through Golden Canyon. The 4km (2 1/2-mile) trail walk takes under two hours, but you need to arrange for a lift back up to the lookout car park.

Joshua Tree National Park

The high Mojave Desert meets the low Colorado Desert here at Joshua Tree.

The park was named after the thousands of spiky, tree-like plants that are actually giant members of the lily family. These 'trees' grow only at altitudes between 914m and 1,524m (3,000–5,000ft) and can reach heights of 12m (40ft).

The most impressive groups of plants are in the high western part of the park.

The road passes by enormous, rounded granite boulders that are scattered through the landscape. These provide a platform for gymnastic displays by rock climbers.

There are three entrances to the park: from Highway 62 at Joshua Tree or Twentynine Palms, and, in the south, via Cottonwood Spring off I-10. The best way to enter the park is from the town of Twentynine Palms. The visitor centre will supply maps and trail guides as well as brochures and general information. There are also visitor centres at Joshua Tree and Cottonwood Spring.

Cholla Cactus Garden

Winding down from the Mojave into the Colorado Desert the landscape changes from rugged rocks and mountains into a barren, flat expanse of parched earth.

The Cholla Cactus Garden is a forest of Opuntia cacti that manages to survive in this harsh environment. One of the prettiest walks in the park passes through here, but be warned: the other name for the cholla is 'jumping cactus', and with good reason; although they do not actually jump, the plants have an annoying tendency to attach themselves to you with even the slightest touch. They rarely grow higher than 1m (3ft), but the length of their spines makes up for their lack of height! Also keep an eye open for the various snakes (including rattlesnakes) that live here, if you want to avoid a potentially nasty encounter.

Zabriskie Point at dawn, Death Valley National Park

Joshua Tree National Park, 74485 National Park Dr, Twentynine Palms. Tel: (760) 367 5500. www.nps.gov. Visitor centres open daily (times vary). Admission charge.

Palm Springs

To anyone in southern California 'the desert' means Palm Springs and its equally affluent neighbours, Rancho Mirage and Palm Desert.

Before the 1920s this was a sleepy little health spa where people came for the hot springs and dry air. Then it was discovered by Hollywood.

Palm Springs rapidly grew to become one of the world's major winter resorts. The skies are always blue, the air always clear, and the golf courses, over 125 of them, always green.

There is even cross-country skiing up on Mount San Jacinto, towering 2,621m (8,600ft) above Palm Springs.

'The Season' for 'the desert' starts in January and continues through to the end of April. To be seen here before Christmas or after Easter is just not done, unless, of course, you want the best rates at hotels and some great travel bargains. The summer can be very hot, but the discounts available can almost make the temperatures bearable. However, many attractions close or have limited hours during the summer. Always telephone in advance.

Moorten Botanical Garden

This 1.6-hectare (4-acre) garden displays over 3,000 different varieties of cactus and other desert plants. You will also see plenty of lizards, birds and dinosaur fossils throughout the garden.
1701 S Palm Canyon Dr, Palm Springs.
Tel: (760) 327 6555.
www.moortengarden.com.
Open: Thur–Tue 10am–4pm.
Admission charge.

Palm Springs Aerial Tramway

A cable-car ride to the summit of **Mount San Jacinto** is one of Palm Springs' most popular attractions. This 1.6km (1-mile)-high ride provides views from Joshua Tree across to the Salton Sea with the whole of the Palm Springs valley in the foreground.

At the top of the mountain, apart from the usual restaurant, bar and souvenir shops, there is a short nature trail, and mules are available for 20-minute rides around the slopes.

Depending upon snow conditions, usually from late November to mid-April, the **Nordic Ski Center** is open for cross-country ski excursions.
Aerial Tramway: tel: (760) 325 1391.
www.pstramway.com. Open: Mon–Fri 10am–8pm, weekends & holidays 8am–8pm. Admission charge.
San Jacinto Ranger Station:
tel: (760) 327 0222.
Nordic Ski Center: tel: (760) 325 3490.

Palm Springs Art Museum

This museum has an eclectic assortment of exhibits from western American art to desert natural history to Indian basketry. It is a collection of considerable regional importance and worth a visit if only for the delightfully landscaped sculpture garden.
101 Museum Dr, Palm Springs.
Tel: (760) 322 4800. www.psmuseum.org.
Open: Tue, Wed & Fri–Sun 10am–5pm, Thur noon–8pm. Closed: Mon.
Admission charge (free on Thur 4–8pm).

Village Green Heritage Center

In the middle of the exclusive shops of **Palm Canyon Drive**, three old buildings from Palm Springs' past look almost too perfect to be genuine.

The McCallum Adobe was built in 1884 and is the town's oldest building. Next door is Cornelia White's 1893

home made from railroad ties, and then there is Ruddy's General Store. This is a re-creation of a typical 1930s general store complete with shelves stocked with over 6,000 genuine items from the period. It is one of the most complete displays of unused general store merchandise in the country.
221 S Palm Canyon Dr, Palm Springs.
Tel: (760) 323 8297.
www.palmsprings.com/history.
Open: Oct–May, Wed & Sun noon–3pm,
Thur–Sat 10am–4pm. Closed: Mon &
Tue. Admission charge.

Palm Desert

This rival of Palm Springs is rapidly becoming one of the desert's major resort towns. The quality of shops along El Paseo is exceptional, equal to that of Rodeo Drive in Los Angeles. The town obviously caters for visitors who do not have to worry too much about money.

Apart from shopping, **The Living Desert** is the other attraction that should not be missed in Palm Desert. This 486-hectare (1,200-acre) garden and wild animal park re-creates eight different desert habitats. There is even a display of nocturnal animals in a special enclosure, plus the option of a camel ride through the desert.
47900 Portola Ave, Palm Desert.
Tel: (760) 346 5694.
www.livingdesert.org. Open: Oct–May
daily 9am–5pm, Jun–Sept daily
8am–1.30pm. Admission charge.

Salton Sea

This vast body of water was formed in 1905 when the Colorado River poured billions of litres of flood water into this desert area that lies below sea level.

There are no natural outlets and over the years evaporation has concentrated the salinity of the water.

It is a major link in the Pacific Flyway, and thousands of birds use the sea either as a stopover or to spend the winter. One-third of all North America's white pelican population winters here.

Nearby Coachella Valley is the centre of the California date growers, and the roads are lined with alternating date-palm groves and shops selling gift-wrapped dates.

Palm Canyon Drive, Palm Springs' main street

California parks

California is blessed with the most diverse scenic national parks in the US. Towering coastal redwoods in the north, bubbling mud at volcanic Mount Lassen, giant rock faces at Yosemite, sand dunes at Death Valley – it would be difficult to imagine a more spectacular collection of natural wonders.

The great Scottish naturalist, John Muir, actively lobbied for the protection of the great mountain wilderness areas of the Sierra Nevada, and, in 1890, Sequoia was the second national park to be created after Yellowstone in Wyoming, and Yosemite was created just a few weeks later. The most recent national park creations were Death Valley and Joshua Tree in the 1990s.

If that were not enough, 526,091 hectares (1.3 million acres) of California have been dedicated to over 270 state parks. Many of these state parks are the equal of their big brother national parks, both in size and variety. Anza-Borrego, on the Mexican border, covers 242,811

Joshua trees at sunset, Mojave National Preserve

El Capitan in winter, Yosemite National Park

hectares (600,000 acres) and several different ecosystems, while Fort Ross on the Northern Sonoma Coast covers just a few hectares, preserving a handful of early 19th-century buildings from Russia's farthest outpost. California's state parks make up the most diverse natural and cultural park system in the nation.

Whether it's lighthouses, vestiges of colonial Russia, Spanish-era adobe buildings or rhododendron reserves, there is something to interest almost everyone. California is the birthplace of mountain biking, and 4,828km (3,000 miles) of hiking, biking and equestrian trails provide never-ending opportunities for adventure. Combine this with 1,006km (625 miles) of lake and river frontage, 451km (280 miles) of coast and 18,000 campsites, and you can spend months here without leaving the state park system.

Central California

From cliff-hugging highways and broad sandy beaches to scattered farms in warm valleys and giant trees in the mountains, Central California has some of the finest scenery and most attractive towns in the state. Spend time in friendly coastal Carmel, visit the famous Hearst Castle and watch eagles soar over the deepest canyons in Sequoia and Kings Canyon National Parks.

Santa Barbara

Santa Barbara is one of the most beautiful towns in the country. It sits on a curving, sandy bay with the Santa Ynez Mountains as a backdrop. Add to this a near-perfect climate and you have the closest an American town gets to paradise.

The Spanish named it *la tierra adorada* – the beloved land. A massive earthquake destroyed the town in 1925 and left the way clear to plan a whole new town based on its Spanish roots. Present-day Santa Barbara is mainly Spanish and mission-style architecture with red tile roofs and a strong Mediterranean flavour. Whitewashed walls and elegant palm trees complete the effect. No wonder it bills itself as 'The American Riviera'.

Indeed, as you stroll along the seafront on a Sunday, taking in the popular Arts and Crafts show, you could be forgiven for thinking you're in the South of France. Add to this a burgeoning wine region, a well-regarded annual film festival, and upmarket hotels such as the renovated Four Seasons Biltmore, and it's easy to see why an increasing number of Hollywood stars are spotted here.

The first stop in Santa Barbara should be the **Visitor Information Center** at 1 Garden Street (*tel: (805) 965 3021. www.santabarbara.com*).

County Courthouse

This Spanish-Moorish castle was built in 1929 and remains the grandest building in town. A visit to the top of the bell tower gives an unparalleled view of Santa Barbara and the bay. *1100 Anacapa St. Tel: (805) 962 6464. www.santabarbaracourthouse.org. Open: Mon–Fri 8am–5pm, Sat & Sun 10am–4.30pm. Free admission.*

Mission Santa Barbara

This is the grandest of the missions established by the Spanish and is often called 'The Queen of Missions'. Founded in 1786, it sits on a knoll high

above the town and its design was based on those of Roman engineers dating back to AD 27. There is a small museum, and the gardens are particularly worth seeing.
2201 Laguna St. Tel: (805) 682 4713. www.santabarbaramission.org. Open: daily 9am–5pm. Admission charge.

Museum of Art
This small but interesting collection covers everything from Roman statues to 20th-century American works. The temporary shows are usually worth a look, too.
1130 State St. Tel: (805) 963 4364. www.sbmuseart.org. Open: Tue–Sun 11am–5pm. Admission charge.

Stearns Wharf
This is the oldest pier on the west coast and is an extension of Santa Barbara's main street, State Street. It was built in 1872 and has the usual mixture of souvenir shops, cafés, restaurants and seafood stands.

San Luis Obispo
An attractive little town that makes a nice break on the drive along Highway 1, San Luis Obispo is known chiefly as the location of California Polytechnic State University (Cal Poly for short). It's also the site of the pretty Mission San Luis Obispo de Tolosa, the fifth mission founded by Junípero Serra, in 1772. If you're in town on a Thursday, visit the farmers' market (6–9pm) between Osos and Nipomo streets.

Mission San Luis Obispo de Tolosa: 751 Palm St. Tel: (805) 781 8220. www.missionsanluisobispo.org. Open: daily 9am–5pm (occasionally closed for special events). Admission charge.

San Simeon
Sixty-four kilometres (40 miles) north of San Luis Obispo, newspaper magnate William Randolph Hearst built what must be the most opulent and extravagant residence in California, if not the nation.

Starting in 1919, **Hearst Castle** took 30 years to build at a cost of three million dollars. Today it is estimated that the building would cost 300 to 400 million dollars to complete.

There are 38 bedrooms, 14 sitting rooms, two libraries, a kitchen and a theatre, and all this is just in the main house (Casa Grande). There are three additional guesthouses.

Santa Barbara County Courthouse

It is the second-biggest attraction in California, after Disneyland®, with over a million visitors a year. Because of its popularity, reservations are essential at the height of the season and are recommended at all times.

Each tour takes 1 hour 45 minutes, and for the first-time visitor Tour 1 is the best introduction. Wear comfortable shoes, as there is a lot of walking to do!

To make reservations call (800) 444 4445. www.hearstcastle.com.
Open: daily, except for New Year's Day, Thanksgiving & Christmas.
Admission charge.

Big Sur

Big Sur is specifically the name of a small town about 32km (20 miles) south of Carmel, but it has come to be synonymous with a section of dramatic coastline that extends from the Carmel Highlands down to San Simeon.

The 145km (90-mile) drive clings precariously to the side of the Santa Lucia Mountains. It is a tortuous two-lane road that takes several hours to drive, but the dramatic scenery more than justifies the journey.

Lookout points are provided all along the route and during the winter months give a bird's-eye view of the California grey whales on their annual migration to and from Mexico. The road passes four state parks and is penetrated by numerous hiking trails.

For many years this was a favourite hideaway for literary giants such as Henry Miller, and Hollywood stars Rita Hayworth and Orson Welles.
Tel: (831) 667 2100.
www.bigsurcalifornia.org

Point Lobos State Reserve

Robert Louis Stevenson wrote that Point Lobos was 'the most beautiful meeting of land and sea on earth'.

This 506-hectare (1,250-acre) state park just south of Carmel is easily accessible by road, but the parking areas are small so in summer it pays to get there early.

Several trails exist in the park, but for a short visit the Cypress Grove Trail will give a good introduction. Look out for the playful sea lions that frolic in the kelp forests off Point Lobos.

Trail maps and wildlife guides are available from the ranger station at the park entrance.
Tel: (831) 624 4909. www.pointlobos.org.
Open: daily 8am–30min after sunset.
Admission charge.

Carmel

This small town by the sea is one of California's biggest tourist attractions.

Originally Carmel was a haven for artists and writers, but they have long since been priced out of the market. The art galleries remain, although the quality varies massively. It is a town that is almost too perfect. There are no neon signs, no traffic lights, no billboards. There is no postal delivery so all 5,000 residents have to collect their mail from the post office.

This effort to remain 'quaint' attracts so many people during the summer, especially at weekends, that it is almost impossible to move. Parking in particular becomes extremely difficult.

There is no denying that Carmel does have considerable charm, but try to avoid weekends. It is a place to visit for ambience rather than sightseeing. The beach is particularly fine (*see pp72–3*), and so is the town's mission.

Mission San Carlos Borromeo del Carmelo

The Carmel Mission was the favourite of Father Junípero Serra, who lies buried in the church. It was the second mission in the chain, built in 1771, and it remained Serra's headquarters until his death. It is located on a splendid site at the mouth of the Carmel River, overlooking the sea.
3080 Rio Rd, Carmel. Tel: (831) 624 1271. www.carmelmission.org. Open: Mon–Sat 9.30am–5pm, Sun 10.30am–5pm. Admission charge.

Mission Carmel, Father Serra's favourite mission

Monterey

In the early years of California, Monterey was the most important city. It was the Spanish capital of Alta California, then the Mexican capital in 1822, and the American capital in 1846.

After the discovery of gold the focus of the state moved north and Monterey became a major fishing port. Today it is tourism that keeps its economy afloat.

Cannery Row

This street of old fish canneries filled with eccentric characters was immortalised by John Steinbeck. Gentrification means it is now just another tourist trap. The aquarium at the far end of the wharf is the one notable exception.
(*See also p79.*)

Fisherman's Wharf

The wharf was built in 1846 as a pier for trading ships coming around Cape Horn. It was also used by sardine fishermen and whaling boats before the fishing industry hit the doldrums.

It has now gone the way of Cannery Row and is little more than a tourists' shopping and restaurant mall. There are, however, good views of the bay from the end of the wharf.

Monterey Bay Aquarium

The importance of this aquarium extends far beyond the Monterey peninsula. It is one of the finest and largest aquariums in the world, with
(*Cont. on p74*)

Walk: Carmel

Carmel is the jewel of the central California coast, and this walk through the town and along the beach will show the best that Carmel has to offer. It is located only 2 hours south of San Francisco.

Allow 2 hours.

The best place to start is at the junction of Dolores St and Ocean Ave. The popularity of Carmel, combined with the limited amount of parking available, is a perennial problem. There is a small public car park at the end of Ocean Ave by the beach and another at Juniper and 3rd.

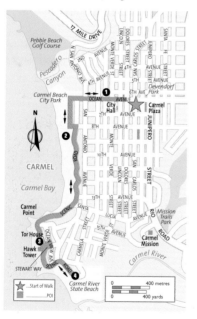

Apart from that, there are 2-hour parking bays on most streets. Fortunately the town is small and nowhere is too far.

1 Ocean Avenue

This is the main shopping street in Carmel, with an enticing collection of boutiques and art galleries. Off Ocean Avenue is a rabbit warren of alleyways and courtyards crammed with even more shops, galleries and restaurants. Carmel has long been associated with the arts.

Walk down Ocean Ave towards the ocean. At the car parking area walk on to the beach and turn left.

2 The beach

The best way to experience this walk to the full is to throw off your shoes and socks and get the sand between your toes. Even during winter the weather can be sunny and warm, and this is one of the best stretches of sand on the coast. The beach sweeps around to the rocks at the southern tip of Carmel Bay.

You do not have to walk on the sand. Scenic Road runs parallel to the beach and it was not named accidentally. It gives unequalled views of the coast.

However, it is better to start on the beach as the first section of Scenic Road does not have a footpath and cars can come perilously close on this narrow street. Scenic Road can be reached from the beach at several points by steps.

The sandy beach ends at a group of surf-spattered rocks at the southern end. *Continue south on the footpath.*

3 Tor House

After a short distance you will see a distinctive house tucked back from the road. Look left and there you will see a medieval-looking house constructed from huge boulders. This was the home of the great American poet, Robinson Jeffers.

To get to the house, turn left up Stewart Way and then left again on to Ocean View Avenue. Tor House is two houses down on the left.

Jeffers built the house and tower with his own hands, hauling the granite stones by horse from the little cove below. The house was modelled after an English Tudor barn and took him less than four years to complete. Jeffers built it using a block and tackle system and wooden planks, similar to methods used by the ancient Egyptians. He lived here from 1919 until his death in 1962. Hawk Tower was built as a retreat for his wife.

Tor House is open for tours on Fridays and Saturdays between 10am and 3pm, strictly by appointment. For reservations *tel: (831) 624 1813 or visit www.torhouse.org. Admission charge. Continue on to the beach.*

4 Carmel River State Beach

This lovely beach features a bird sanctuary. It can get windswept, however, and, like Carmel's other beach, is unsuitable for swimming. *Return to Ocean Ave by the same route.*

A walker's view of Tor House, Carmel

over 35,000 plants and animals. (*See also p79.*)
886 Cannery Row, Monterey. Tel: (831) 648 4800. www.montereybay aquarium.org. Open: daily 10am–6pm. Admission charge.

Monterey's Path of History

A dozen historic buildings are on the walking tour through the oldest parts of Monterey. Entrance tickets can be bought at any of the buildings, and the ticket gives admission to all of them.

The Custom House at 1 Custom House Plaza is the most logical place to start. Right by Fisherman's Wharf, this important building is the oldest government office on the whole Pacific

The harbour at Monterey Bay

coast, and it was here that the US flag was first raised in 1846.
Maps of the self-guiding tour are available with ticket purchase. For opening times call (831) 649 7118.

Municipal Wharf

A small fishing fleet still uses this last working wharf in Monterey and it is an ideal place to capture something of the flavour of the old Monterey of Steinbeck's time.

Sequoia and Kings Canyon National Parks

Even when Yosemite National Park is as packed as a suburban shopping mall, Kings Canyon and Sequoia National Parks to the south are relatively unruffled. Contiguous and equal to each other in grandeur, Kings Canyon primarily pays homage to the High Sierra wilderness of Kings River country, while Sequoia shows off its

JOHN STEINBECK

Most of Steinbeck's writings were based on Monterey or Salinas, where he was born in 1902. To support himself through Stanford University, which he attended intermittently between 1919 and 1926, he worked as a labourer. His first novel to achieve popular success, *Tortilla Flat*, was based on real-life experiences with the agricultural workers of Monterey County.

The Grapes of Wrath was published in 1937, and in the same year appeared as both a stage play and a film. The book won a Pulitzer Prize and established Steinbeck as a major American writer.

Several books followed, including *Of Mice and Men*, *Cannery Row* and *East of Eden*, but none reached the critical success of his work in the 1930s. In spite of this, in 1962 he was awarded the Nobel Prize for Literature.

After spending most of his life in California, he died in New York in 1968.

stands of Giant Sequoia. Though Kings Canyon has big trees, those at Sequoia's Giant Forest are incomparable. The lowest limb of the 'General Sherman', for example, is 2m (7ft) across and would create a canopy for a 12-storey building.

Activities abound in both parks, including hiking, horse riding and skiing. There's also potholing at Crystal Cave near Giant Forest and at Boyden Cavern between Grant Grove and Cedar Grove, although for the less adventurous, guided tours of both are available (for Crystal Cave, buy tickets in advance at Lodgepole or Foothills visitor centres; for Boyden Cavern, buy tickets at the cave itself).

For more information on both parks, contact Sequoia & Kings Canyon National Parks, 47050 Generals Hwy, Three Rivers, CA 93271 (*tel: (559) 565 3341; www.nps.gov*). In addition, there are five visitor centres in the parks, the biggest of which is the **Foothills Visitor Center** (*tel: (559) 565 3135*). Both parks also contain campsites; a few accept reservations in advance (*tel: (877) 444 6777; www.recreation.gov*); others are on a first-come, first-served basis.

Note that there are no petrol stations in either park, and that warnings about storing food in bear-resistant lockers are particularly stringent here and must be taken seriously.

White Mountains

An all-day journey at best, a side-trip via Highway 168 from Big Pine east to the stark White Mountains and the Bristlecone Pine Forest is well worth the effort. Here stand the most ancient living things on earth, scattered groves of gnarled *Pinus longaeva* or bristlecone pine trees. Many of these sturdy, scruffy, and seemingly dead trees are estimated to be more than 4,000 years old. The area is desolate, so start with a full tank of petrol and bring your own water and food (campsites are available).

White Mountain Ranger Station (US Forest Service), 798 N Main St, Bishop, CA 93514. Tel: (760) 873 2500.

Mount Whitney and environs

Not for solitude do visitors climb to the top of Mount Whitney, highest peak in the continental US outside Alaska. During the snow-free season (mid-July to early Oct) the 16km (10-mile) trail to the top can become dangerously overcrowded, so there is a lottery for climbing permits – *see www.fs.fed.us* for details of climbing and backpacking permits.

An interesting aside between the mountain and the town is the **Alabama Hills**, a dirt-road detour through enormous granite boulders, perhaps familiar as backdrops for Westerns such as *High Sierra, Bad Day at Black Rock* and *They Died With Their Boots On*. More fascinating is the fact that quite close to Mount Whitney, via Highway 136 southeast from Lone Pine, is **Death Valley National Park**, the lowest point in North America (*see pp59–62*).

Tour: 17-Mile Drive, Pebble Beach

This is a tour of Pebble Beach, an exclusive residential development set amid forests and golf courses by a fabulously beautiful coastline. The 17-Mile Drive was originally named after the horse-drawn carriage ride from the Hotel Del Monte in Monterey out to the Del Monte Forest.

Allow 1½ hours.

The drive can be started at either the southern entrance at the Carmel Gate on Ocean Avenue or in the north at the Pacific Grove Gate on Sunset Drive. It is virtually impossible to get lost as the

whole drive is very well signposted. Pebble Beach is a private estate and a toll is charged for using the road.
Start at the Carmel Gate and turn right on to the 17-Mile Drive. Follow the signs.

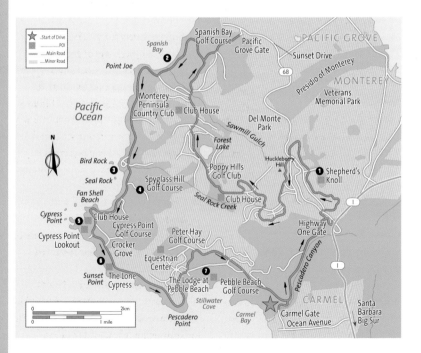

1 Shepherd's Knoll

This high point on the drive gives sweeping views of Monterey Bay and the San Gablian Mountains.

The road passes through the Del Monte Forest and hillsides covered with huckleberry bushes. Nestled in the woods are the luxurious homes of some of California's wealthiest families.

2 Spanish Bay and the Restless Sea

In 1769, Juan Gaspar de Portolá camped here while trying to locate Monterey Bay; today it is the perfect spot to have a picnic and watch the waves crash.

A walking trail along the coastal bluff starts here and continues past some of Monterey Bay's richest tidepools.

3 Seal and Bird Rocks

These landmark offshore rocks are home to a huge colony of shoreline birds, particularly the double-crested cormorant. There is also a large population of California sea lions and harbour seals that can be heard barking in the distance.

4 Spyglass Hill Golf Course

This is one of seven golf courses at Pebble Beach and is considered one of the best in the US. It is said that Robert Louis Stevenson was inspired by the view from this, his favourite hill, while writing *Treasure Island*. Each of the course's 18 holes takes its name from this classic.

A view of shoreline and surf near Pebble Beach on the 17-Mile Drive

As you drive by, it is not unusual to see deer sharing the course with golfers.

5 Cypress Point Lookout

The lookout gives one of the finest views of the coastline on 17-Mile Drive. On a clear day you can see as far as Point Sur Lighthouse (32km/20 miles).

Immediately below the lookout is a breeding area for harbour seals, and in the spring the newborn seal pups can be watched from above.

6 The Lone Cypress

This solitary cypress clinging to an apparently bare rock has become one of California's most familiar landmarks.

7 The Lodge at Pebble Beach

This famous resort, built in 1919, offers deluxe accommodation and restaurants with sweeping views of the ocean.

Walk: Cannery Row and Pacific Grove

Cannery Row was immortalised by John Steinbeck's book of the same name. This walk combines lovely coastal scenery with great marine wildlife viewing and passes through some of the most historic sections of Monterey.

Allow 2 hours, excluding a visit to the aquarium.

Start at the car park for Fisherman's Wharf off Del Monte Ave.

1 Fisherman's Wharf

This prime sightseeing attraction no longer attracts many fishermen.

Commercial fishing is now based on the Municipal Wharf and the original Fisherman's Wharf is little more than a collection of souvenir shops and tourist restaurants. A couple of fish and crab stands still operate, but

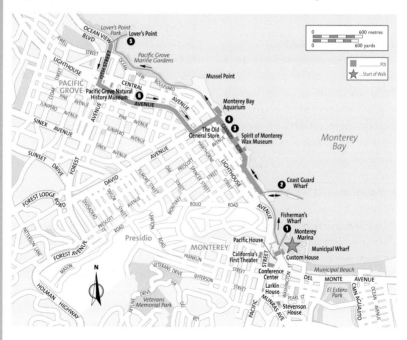

they have been joined by ice-cream stands and tourist shops. Boat tours and whale-watching trips are also offered.

If you make your way down to the end of the wharf you will be rewarded with excellent views of the harbour and Monterey Bay from the observation deck.
Turn right on to the footpath as soon as you leave Fisherman's Wharf and walk through Fisherman's Shoreline Park to the Coast Guard Wharf.

2 Coast Guard Wharf

In the winter months take the time to walk out to the end of the pier. Every year hundreds of California sea lions congregate here, and you can watch them basking in the sun from a few metres away.
Leaving the wharf, turn right on to Cannery Row, and follow it to the end.

3 Cannery Row

John Steinbeck knew and wrote about a very different Cannery Row to the one that now exists. Gone are the stinking fish canneries. They have been replaced by attractions such as the Steinbeck's Spirit of Monterey Wax Museum.

The Row is now full of souvenir shops, restaurants and then more souvenir shops.

4 Monterey Bay Aquarium

This wonderful state-of-the-art aquarium is devoted exclusively to the marine life of Monterey Bay. At its heart and making up the centrepiece of the aquarium is a three-storey giant kelp forest that encapsulates life in the Bay.

There is also a popular sea otter tank, numerous tidepool and touching exhibits as well as outdoor observation decks. The self-service café is excellent, offering fare that is way above what you'll find on Cannery Row.
From the aquarium follow the trail to Lover's Point in Pacific Grove. The trail overlooks the wild, rocky scenery of Monterey Bay.

5 Lover's Point

Pacific Grove is famous for the thousands of monarch butterflies that migrate through here every winter. The town is then transformed into 'Butterfly Town, USA'. A butterfly sculpture prominently displayed in the small park on this promontory sticking out into the bay serves as a year-long reminder of that event.
Take 17th St for two blocks and turn left on to Lighthouse Ave.

6 Lighthouse Avenue

Seventeenth Street enters Lighthouse Avenue in the middle of Pacific Grove's busy shopping area. A wide street lined with many interesting shops and some fine Victorian architecture, it has lots of charm.
At David Avenue, turn left and head back down to Cannery Row.

Missions

In 1769, when Father Junípero Serra was already 55, he travelled 1,200km (750 miles) by donkey, from Mexico to San Diego, to build the first of a series of missions that would eventually extend up the coast of California as far as Sonoma to the north of San Francisco.

Junípero Serra had moved to Mexico from his birthplace in Mallorca when he was 37. He was a small man with a pronounced limp, the result of an injury in Mexico for which he refused to have treatment. At the time of his death in 1784 he had travelled thousands of kilometres and established a further nine missions in what were then the remote outposts of California. He is buried in the second mission he founded, at Carmel.

Serra was succeeded by Fermín Francisco de Lasuén who, like Serra, had moved to Mexico in his 30s. He

Mission San Luis Obispo, Father Junípero Serra's fifth in the chain

The mission at Carmel

established an additional eight missions during his 18 years in the office of president of the missions, and he was already 66 years old when he started the project. It was de Lasuén who developed the style of architecture that has come to be known throughout California as the mission style.

The missions were linked by El Camino Real – the Royal Road. Streets bearing the same name, following the original route, can be found in most of California's coastal towns today.

All of California's missions are open to the public.

Northern California

From the sparsely populated border with Oregon in the north to the high-tech urban civilisation to the south, Northern California has vast areas of wilderness, preserved Gold Rush history and striking coastlines. Discover rural volcanic landscapes speckled with caves, dense forests that are home to the tallest trees on earth, ghost towns reliving their rich mining past and one of the world's great cities: San Francisco.

SAN FRANCISCO

San Francisco is everyone's favourite city. Its visual appeal has a lot to do with this. It is built on a series of hills that not only help to create an interesting architectural environment but also allow glimpses of San Francisco Bay, the Golden Gate Bridge and the Pacific Ocean, as the city itself is surrounded on three sides by water.

This spectacular location on a peninsula adds further to San Francisco's charm. The city is small. It covers only 119sq km (46sq miles) and has a population of less than 800,000. The scale is human, and it is one of the few North American cities that is both pleasant and manageable to walk around.

The climate helps its reputation too. It rarely gets too hot and almost never freezes. Natural air conditioning keeps the air clean and sparkling for most of the time. It does, however, get cold, particularly in the summer when the famous sea fogs roll in from the Pacific.

Just because it is August in California does not mean it is hot in San Francisco.

Within two years of James Marshall discovering gold in the Sierra Nevada, San Francisco grew from a population of 900 to 25,000. Forty years later it was over 300,000.

This cosmopolitan population, drawn by the lure of gold, set the pattern for the future. It is an international community with a great deal of tolerance. The city has one of the largest Asian populations outside Asia, a Chinatown bigger than many towns in China, and large Japanese, Vietnamese and Filipino communities. Then there are the Mexicans. The Mission District is dominated by Spanish-speaking families from Mexico and Central America. You can spend a day there without hearing a word of English. The Italians still have a very strong presence, although their traditional neighbourhood of North Beach is slowly being absorbed by Chinatown.

For well over a century San Francisco has retained its ethnic diversity, and its legendary tolerance has embraced the Beatniks of the 50s, the flower children of the 60s and now the largest gay population in the US.

Many of these factors have led to an active and progressive cultural scene. The opera and symphony orchestra are both of international standing. Both mainstream and experimental theatre are thriving. Many of the great 20th-century artists such as Mark Rothko and Clyfford Still made their home here.

Most long-time residents rarely think of earthquakes, although the 1989 Loma Prieta shock jolted many people out of their complacency. All modern buildings have to be built to very rigorous standards and are considered to be virtually earthquake-proof. Even many of the older buildings have withstood severe shocks, including the 1906 disaster. Fire has always been a bigger danger than the actual quake. In spite of the 1906 earthquake and several major fires, old San Francisco has remained remarkably well preserved. The old, painted Victorian houses have lost none of their charm, even if they tend to be in some of the less desirable neighbourhoods. The cable cars still clank along as a living relic from the past, and Golden Gate Bridge commands the entrance to the bay as it has for the past 70 years.

People who have never visited California often speak of Los Angeles and San Francisco in the same breath, though in reality the two cities could not be more dissimilar, whether geographically, culturally or politically.

Cable cars

The first cable car ran in San Francisco in 1873, and at one time there were eight lines with over 177km (110 miles) of track. Today only three lines and 18km (11 miles) of track remain, but the cable car has continued to keep its popularity.

The cable car does not have any form of power of its own. It moves by attaching a clamp to an endlessly moving cable below the tracks. To stop,

A cable car in downtown San Francisco

Northern California

San Francisco

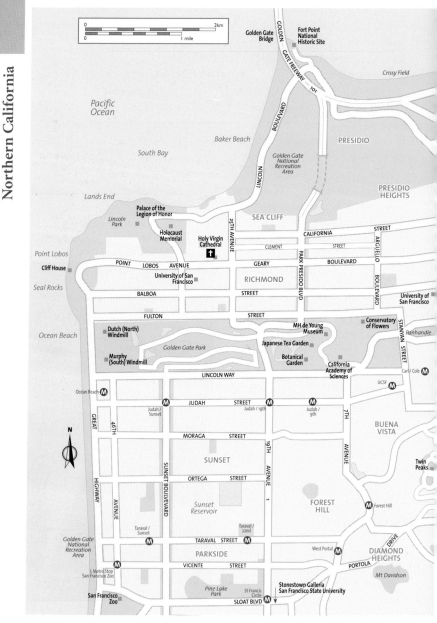

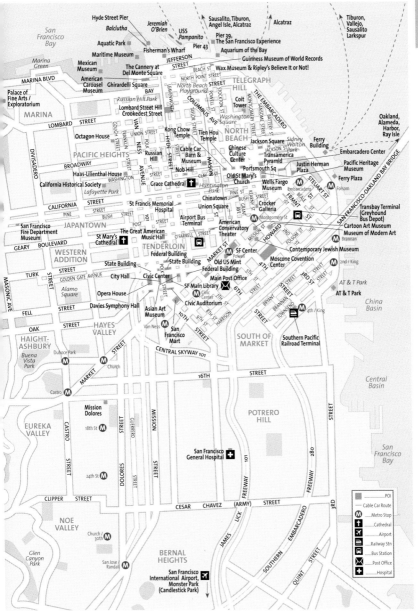

Hyde Street Pier
Balclutha
Jeremiah O'Brien
USS Pampanito
Pier 39, The San Francisco Experience
Sausalito, Tiburon, Angel Isle, Alcatraz
Alcatraz
Tiburon, Vallejo, Sausalito Larkspur
Aquatic Park
Fisherman's Wharf
Pier 43
Maritime Museum
Aquarium of the Bay
Guinness Museum of World Records
Wax Museum & Ripley's Believe It or Not!
JEFFERSON STREET
BEACH ST
Mexican Museum
The Cannery at Del Monte Square
American Carousel Museum
Ghirardelli Square
BAY
NORTH POINT STREET
North Beach Playground
North Beach STREET
Palace of Fine Arts / Exploratorium
Russian Hill Park
Lombard Street Hill
Crookedest Street
COLUMBUS AVE
Coit Tower
Washington Square
TELEGRAPH HILL
THE EMBARCADERO
Oakland, Alameda, Harbor, Ray Isle
MARINA
LOMBARD STREET
Octagon House
Kong Chow Temple
Tien Hou Temple
NORTH BEACH
STOCKTON STREET
POWELL STREET
MASON STREET
TAYLOR STREET
Jackson Square
Sidney Walton Park
Ferry Building
MARINA BLVD
Marina Green
DIVISADERO
VAN NESS
COLUMBUS AVE
Cable Car Barn & Museum
Chinese Culture Center
JACKSON ST
Transamerica Pyramid
Embarcadero Center
Pacific Heritage Museum
Ferry Plaza
PACIFIC HEIGHTS
Russian Hill
HYDE STREET
UNION STREET
BROADWAY
Nob Hill
Old St Mary's Church
Portsmouth Sq
Justin Herman Plaza
Haas-Lilienthal House
WASHINGTON
Grace Cathedral
Huntington Park
Wells Fargo Museum
Folsom
California Historical Society
Lafayette Park
Chinatown
CLAY STREET
PINE ST
Crocker Galleria
SAN FRANCISCO-OAKLAND BAY BRIDGE
CALIFORNIA STREET
PINE STREET
BUSH STREET
St Francis Memorial Hospital
Union Square
GRANT AVE
BUSH ST
STEUART ST
FREMONT ST
San Francisco Fire Department Museum
JAPANTOWN
POST STREET
The Great American Music Hall
Airport Bus Terminal
American Conservatory Theater
Montgomery St
1ST ST
2ND ST
HOWARD ST
FOLSOM ST
Transbay Terminal (Greyhound Bus Depot)
Cartoon Art Museum
Museum of Modern Art
WESTERN ADDITION
St Mary's Cathedral
O'FARRELL STREET
SF Center
MISSION ST
Brannan
GEARY BOULEVARD
Federal Building
Powell
Moscone Convention Center
Contemporary Jewish Museum
TURK STREET
State Building
State Building
Federal Building
4TH STREET
2nd / King
GOLDEN GATE AVENUE
City Hall
Old US Mint
3RD ST
AT & T Park
FELL STREET
Opera House
Civic Center
Main Post Office
BRYANT STREET
AT & T Park
China Basin
OAK STREET
Davies Symphony Hall
SF Main Library
Civic Center
Civic Auditorium
BRANNAN STREET
TOWNSEND STREET
4th/King
HAYES VALLEY
Asian Art Museum
Van Ness
10TH STREET
9TH ST
8TH ST
HARRISON
SOUTH OF MARKET
Southern Pacific Railroad Terminal
HAIGHT-ASHBURY
Buena Vista Park
Duboce Park
San Francisco Mart
CENTRAL SKYWAY 101
Church
Castro
MARKET STREET
16TH STREET
STREET
Central Basin
EUREKA VALLEY
CASTRO STREET
Mission Dolores
18th St
GUERRERO STREET
DOLORES STREET
MISSION STREET
POTRERO HILL
STREET
San Francisco Bay
24th St
San Francisco General Hospital
101 FREEWAY
LICK FREEWAY
280 FREEWAY
CLIPPER STREET
CESAR CHAVEZ (ARMY) STREET
NOE VALLEY
Church / 30th
JAMES
SOUTHERN
EMBARCADERO
3RD
Glen Canyon Park
San Jose / Randall
BERNAL HEIGHTS
San Francisco International Airport, Monster Park (Candlestick Park)
QUINT STREET

San Francisco Bay
San Francisco Bay

POI
Cable Car Route
Metro Stop
Cathedral
Airport
Railway Stn
Bus Station
Post Office
Hospital

the brakeman releases the clamp and applies the brakes. To move, he reattaches the clamp. At the end of the line the car must be turned around on a turntable and the passengers are often invited to lend some force to the task.

The quaint, clanking cars are as good a way to travel as any on San Francisco's congested streets, and the three operating lines cover several well-known tourist haunts. The Powell-Mason and Powell-Hyde lines both depart from the Powell Street turnaround at Powell and Market, and run to Fisherman's Wharf. The third, the California Line, goes along California Street between Market Street and Van Ness Avenue.

During the summer be prepared for long queues. It is best to buy tickets before boarding, and there are machines at the terminals and major stops.

To find out more about the history and workings of cable cars, visit the **Cable Car Museum** on Mason Street. This is the main control centre, where you can see the actual cables running at precisely 15.3km/h (9$\frac{1}{2}$ mph) over 4m (14ft) pulleys called sheaves. There is also a good exhibition of old photographs, drawings and models, and some of the original cars built in 1873 by Andrew Hallidie.
Cable Car Museum, 1201 Mason St. Tel: (415) 474 1887.
www.cablecarmuseum.org.
Open: daily 10am–6pm in summer, 10am–5pm in winter. Free admission.

Alcatraz

Until its closure in 1963, The Rock, now administered by the National Parks Service, was home to some of America's most notorious criminals.

Most of the original cells, the hospital and dining room are open, and a self-guiding tour is available with a tape-recorded commentary by former inmates and guards.

This is one of the most popular attractions in San Francisco, so make your ferry bookings as far ahead as possible. Remember to take some warm clothing and wear comfortable shoes.
Ferries leave from Pier 33 starting at 9.30am, with the last boat leaving at 5pm in the summer and 2pm in the winter. The Night Tour operates all year Thur–Mon evenings. www.nps.gov (tickets: tel: (415) 981 7625. www.alcatrazcruises.com).

California Palace of the Legion of Honor

This neoclassical building was built in 1924 by the sugar millionaire Spreckels family, to honour the dead of World War I. The building was donated to the city and now houses a huge and impressive collection of European art. There is a fine collection of Rodin sculptures, including an original casting of *The Thinker* dominating the entrance.
Lincoln Park, at 34th Ave & Clement St. Tel: (415) 750 3600. www.famsf.org. Open: Tue–Sun 9.30am–5.15pm. Closed: Mon. Admission charge (free first Tue of every month).

The neoclassical Palace of the Legion of Honor

Chinatown

This is one of the largest Chinese settlements outside Asia, and although many Chinese immigrants have moved out to Richmond and elsewhere, there is still an authentic community here. Immigration started during the Gold Rush days when Chinese railway workers were brought over to construct the Transcontinental Railway. They were segregated into a ghetto that became known as Chinatown in the 1850s.

Today the Chinese population spreads way beyond the 24-city-block area of Chinatown, and only a quarter of the city's Chinese population lives there. However, Chinatown is still the true cultural and political focus of the community.

Grant Avenue forms the main street, and you enter through a gateway on Bush Street guarded by stone lions. It is the oldest street in the city and is always busy and congested, as you would expect for the most densely populated neighbourhood in San Francisco. Shops filled with cheap oriental souvenirs rub shoulders with

(*Cont. on p90*)

Tour: 49-Mile Drive

If you only have one day to see San Francisco, then take this drive. It passes virtually every major sight in the city. Where you start is not important, though it is better to plan the drive so that you avoid the congested downtown area during rush hours.

Allow 3 hours.

The route is marked with '49-Mile Drive' blue-and-white seagull signs, but they are erratic and it is easy to miss them.

From Union Square take Post St to Grant Ave, turn left and drive through the Chinatown Gate to California St.

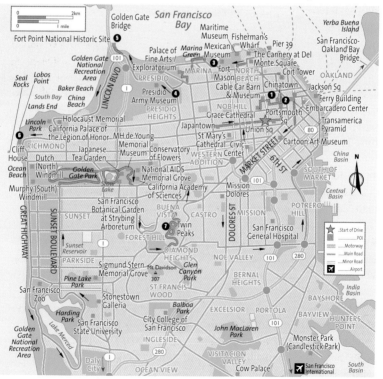

1 Chinatown

The junction of California and Grant is the heart of Chinatown. Cable cars run along this section of San Francisco – they always have right of way.

Continue up to Nob Hill, pass between the Mark Hopkin's Hotel on the left and the Fairmont on the right. Continue past the Flood Mansion and turn right in front of Grace Cathedral on to Taylor St. Turn right on to Washington St and the Cable Car Barn is on the left at the junction with Mason St. Follow the signs as far as Kearny St.

2 Portsmouth Square

A lift from the car park goes straight into Portsmouth Square. This is the social centre of Chinatown.

Turn left on to Kearny, follow the signs as far as Lombard St, and turn left. Coit Tower is a short detour to the right. Follow the signs, pass Pier 39 and drive along Fisherman's Wharf to Ghiradelli Square. Take Bay St to Marina Blvd.

3 Fort Mason

This collection of old warehouses is now home to over 30 non-profit groups, and the Museo ItalioAmericano.

Follow the signs through the Marina District, pass the Palace of Fine Arts and enter the Presidio on Lincoln Blvd.

4 The Presidio

Established by the Spanish in 1776 and taken over by the United States in 1846, these 583 hectares (1,440 acres) of wooded hills are an army base. There

are walking and biking tours in the grounds – see *www.nps.gov* for details. *Continue on Lincoln Blvd and turn off at Long Ave.*

5 Fort Point

At the end of the road nestling under the Golden Gate Bridge is Fort Point, the only brick fort west of the Mississippi. *Return to Lincoln Blvd and continue to the end. In Lincoln Park pass the California Palace of the Legion of Honor and turn right on Point Lobos Ave.*

6 Cliff House

The Cliff House has a restaurant and bistro and great views of Seal Rock. *The road passes the wide expanse of Ocean Beach and hugs the coast until it passes the Zoo on the left, and continues around Lake Merced where it turns north and follows Sunset Blvd to Golden Gate Park. Follow the signs on the meandering route through the park and climb up to the summit of Twin Peaks.*

7 Twin Peaks

The 277m (910ft) summit offers a 360-degree panorama of San Francisco. *Continue down across Market St to Dolores St. Pass Mission Dolores on the right and continue through the Mission District to Potrero Hill. Take Highway 280 north to the 6th St exit. Follow Howard St to the Embarcadero Center and follow the signs through the Financial District down Market St to the Civic Center, on to Japantown and return to Union Square down Post St.*

restaurants, jade merchants, herb shops and fortune cookie factories.

To see where the Chinese shop, leave Grant Avenue and wander along **Stockton Street** any morning and join the shoppers hunting for the freshest exotic vegetables or maybe buying a live chicken from a stall on the street. Stroll through **Portsmouth Square** at any time of day and watch the old men playing mah-jong and chess. In the early morning this is a popular place to practise t'ai chi exercises.

All this exotic colour cries out to be photographed, but be careful. Many of the people here strongly dislike having their photograph taken, so be discreet or ask permission first.

There are two small museums that can help put Chinatown into historical perspective. **The Chinese Historical Society of America** documents the history of the Chinese in California. It has a large collection of Chinese American artefacts, and hosts interesting temporary exhibitions (*965 Clay St; tel: (415) 391 1188; www.chsa.org; open: Tue–Fri noon–5pm, Sat 11am–4pm; admission charge*). **The Chinese Culture Center**, located on the third floor of the Hilton hotel, has regular exhibitions and also organises walking tours (*750 Kearny St; tel: (415) 986 1822; www.c-c-c.org; open: Tue–Sat 10am–4pm; free admission*).

A few temples remain that are worth a visit. The most important is the **Tien Hou Temple** on the top floor of 125 Waverly Place, which dates back to the Gold Rush days.

Civic Center
Sitting in the triangle formed by the arteries of Van Ness Avenue and Market Street, this assembly of administrative offices, arts venues and public spaces reflects the civic zeal that erupted after the 1906 earthquake.

Asian Art Museum
The former San Francisco Public Library has been transformed into a museum dedicated to Oriental art. Based on the 12,000-piece collection of former Olympic Committee president Avery Brundage covering 6,000 years, 2,500 objects are on display at any time. There is a remarkable collection of Buddhist art from India, Tibet and Nepal; magnificent examples of Chinese lacquer-work and ebony carving; and the largest collection of jade in the western hemisphere, with over 1,200 pieces.
200 Larkin St. Tel: (415) 581 3500. www.asianart.org. Open: Tue–Sun 10am–5pm. Admission charge (free first Sun of every month).

City Hall
Designed by Arthur Brown Jr and John Bakewell Jr in 1915, City Hall epitomises the vogue for the Beaux-Arts style rampant at that time. Its neo-Baroque dome is modelled on St Peter's in Rome.

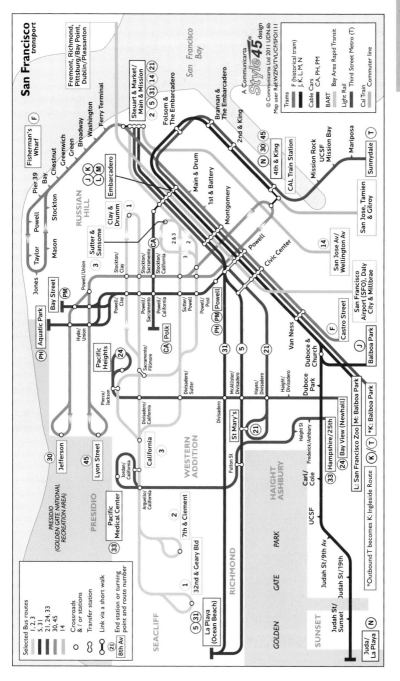

Northern California

Earthquakes

The catastrophic events of 1906 linger in the minds of visitors to the Golden State, but Californian residents rarely think about earthquakes – until a big one happens. Fortunately this is not a common occurrence, though rather more common than a lot of Californians would like to believe. Eighty per cent of the population lives on a series of fault lines that include the infamous San Andreas Fault. Earthquakes of varying magnitude are common throughout the state but they are usually too minor to feel, never mind cause damage.

In the 1940s Charles Richter at the California Institute of Technology devised the measurement of energy released by an earthquake. The scale is logarithmic, with each number on the scale representing a ten-fold increase in ground vibration. Since 1980, 24 earthquakes with a magnitude of 5.5 and above have

Earthquake trail near the Bear Valley Visitors' Center, Point Reyes National Seashore, just north of San Francisco

A dramatic aerial view of the San Andreas Fault

caused several billion dollars' worth of damage in the state. The biggest was the Loma Prieta that shook the San Francisco Bay area with a 7.1 magnitude jolt in 1989, resulting in 63 deaths, 3,757 injuries and a $6 billion bill. It was the worst disaster for San Francisco since the great earthquake and fire of 1906.

An earthquake happens when the earth's tectonic plates, which are continually sliding past each other, meet an obstruction, causing a build-up of tension that is suddenly released. The San Andreas Fault lies along the junction of the Pacific plate and North American plate, which move past each other at about 6cm (2in) a year. In 1906, the release of tension along this fault created an earthquake that measured 8.3 on the Richter scale and devastated San Francisco.

The San Andreas Fault runs from the Imperial Valley in the southeast of the state to Mendocino on the northern coast, and the whole state is criss-crossed by a multitude of lesser fault lines. Every day hundreds of small quakes shake seismographs but barely make a ripple in a glass of water.

The best place to see the San Andreas Fault is 48km (30 miles) north of San Francisco at Point Reyes. The National Park Service has developed an earthquake trail where visitors can actually walk along the San Andreas fault line and witness the magnitude of the 1906 disaster.

Coit Tower bathed in evening sunshine

San Francisco Main Library

Built in 1996, this brilliant-white building replaced the original 1917 building that was damaged in the 1989 earthquake.
100 Larkin St at Grove St. Tel: (415) 557 4400. www.sfpl.org. Library open: Tue–Thur 9am–8pm, Fri noon–6pm, Sat 10am–6pm, Sun noon–5pm, Mon 10am–6pm. Free admission.

San Francisco War Memorial & Performing Arts Center

The San Francisco Opera moved to this grand neoclassical building in 1923. The city is well known for its tradition of fine opera, and the great Enrico Caruso sang here the night before the 1906 earthquake.

401 Van Ness Ave. Tel (415) 621 6600. www.sfwmpac.org. Tours are offered every hour Mon only, 10am–2pm. Admission charge.

United Nations Plaza

East of Hyde Street is the United Nations Plaza, where there is an equestrian statue of Simón Bolívar, the liberator of South America. The name of the plaza commemorates the signing of the UN Charter in 1945 in the nearby War Memorial Opera House. A small farmers' market takes place here every Wednesday and Sunday. A short detour to 7th and Mission streets takes you to the striking new Federal Building.

Coit Tower

The tower was built in 1933 as a memorial to volunteer firemen, with a bequest from Lillie Hitchcock Coit, a 19th-century eccentric who chased fire engines. The Pioneer Park car park below the tower gives good views of the bay. Even better, take a lift to the observation deck at the top of the tower.

Inside are 16 fantastic murals created as part of a make-work project during the 1930s depression.
Telegraph Hill. Tel: (415) 362 0808. Open: daily 10am–6pm. Admission charge.

Financial District

As its name implies, this is the major commercial centre of San Francisco.

555 California Street

Formerly the Bank of America Center, this massive black structure is an obvious display of wealth, power and self-importance. A 200-ton black granite sculpture, *Transcendence*, by Masayuki Nagare sits within the plaza. While it resembles a liver, it is locally known as the Banker's Heart.

Embarcadero Center

This distinctive group of buildings houses a three-level shopping mall, offices and a Meridien hotel.

The underground car park usually has spaces; some local restaurants offer validation, which reduces the rates and makes it free at weekends from 10am to noon and from 5pm to midnight during the week ($5 minimum purchase).
www.embarcaderocenter.com

Ferry Building Marketplace

The landmark clock tower withstood the 1906 earthquake, and the renovated Ferry Building has become the city's mecca for foodies. There are gourmet shops and restaurants inside and a farmers' market outside on Tuesdays (*10am–2pm*), Thursdays (*10am–2pm*) and Saturdays (*8am–2pm*).
One Ferry Building. Tel: (415) 983 8030. www.ferrybuildingmarketplace.com. Open daily, hours vary.

Pacific Heritage Museum

This small museum focuses on the contributions that Pacific Rim immigrants have made to the state.

The building is located on the site of San Francisco's original mint. Now carefully restored, it has a basement exhibition showing the original vaults.
608 Commercial St. Tel: (415) 399 1124. Open: Tue–Sat 10am–4pm. Closed: Sun & Mon. Free admission.

Wells Fargo History Museum

Full of memorabilia from the early days of the company, including a restored, nine-passenger stagecoach, the main theme of the museum is the Gold Rush and Wells Fargo's participation.
420 Montgomery St, San Francisco. Tel: (415) 396 2619. www.wellsfargohistory.com. Open: Mon–Fri 9am–5pm. Closed: Sat & Sun. Free admission.

Fisherman's Wharf

Native San Franciscans dismiss Fisherman's Wharf as one big tourist trap. They may be right, but if you can overlook the amusement arcade, museums and plethora of T-shirt and seashell jewellery shops, there are still a few authentic corners.

A small fishing fleet still operates out of the harbour at the foot of Jones Street. Their catch is sold to the local restaurants, and at the junction of Jefferson and Taylor streets Italian merchants still operate crab stands selling freshly cooked Dungeness crab and sourdough bread. For the old flavour of this part of town, walk along Pier 45, which is still a working wharf.

(*Cont. on p98*)

Walk: San Francisco waterfront

This walk combines some of the best views of the Bay with several major tourist sites, plus good shopping, street entertainment and great food.

Allow 1 hour, plus sights.

Start from the Pier 39 multi-storey car park between the Embarcadero and North Point. There is usually space available here, and with validation from one of Pier 39's restaurants the parking fee is quite reasonable.

1 Pier 39

This old steamship wharf is now a two-level shopping and restaurant complex. The street performers here provide free entertainment, and the views from the end of the pier are some of the best of

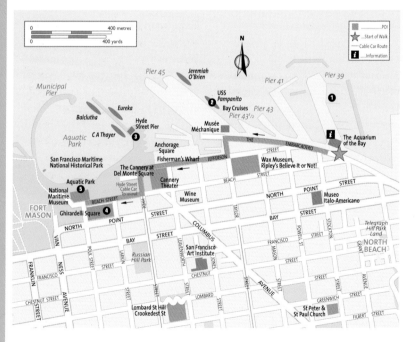

the bay. Between September and May, hundreds of California sea lions can be seen from the viewing area at K Dock. *www.pier39.com.*

From Pier 39 continue west along the Embarcadero, keeping as close to the waterfront as possible.

2 USS *Pampanito*

This restored World War II fleet submarine, a veteran of six Pacific patrols, sits at Pier 45. Also here is the World War II liberty ship *Jeremiah O'Brien*, and the wonderfully old-fashioned **Musée Mécanique**, home to hundreds of coin-operated machines (*www.maritime.org; www.musee mechanique.org*).

Continue along the waterfront by Pier 45, which still has a small working fishing fleet. Continue along Jefferson St, past the Cannery complex on the left.

3 Hyde Street Pier

On the right-hand side of the street as it opens out into Aquatic Park is Hyde Street Pier, which is part of the National Maritime Museum. Several historic ships are anchored here, including the *Eureka*, an 1890 ferryboat; the *Balclutha*, a Scottish merchant ship built in 1886; and a three-masted schooner, *CA Thayer*, that carried timber down the California coast.

The San Francisco Maritime National Historical Park is the official name of this area. Stop in at the lovely visitor centre at the corner of Jefferson and Hyde streets (*www.nps.gov*).

Ghirardelli Square

Walk up Hyde St past the cable-car turntable and turn right on to Beach. There are good views out over Aquatic Park. Continue to Larkin St.

4 Ghirardelli Square

At the junction of Larkin and Beach is one of San Francisco's most popular developments (*see p98*).
*900 N Point St. Tel: (415) 775 5500. www.ghirardellisq.com.
Return to Beach St and turn left.*

5 National Maritime Museum

Opposite Ghirardelli Square, the National Maritime Museum has a display of model ships, photographs and various nautical memorabilia. It is currently undergoing construction so access is limited.
Beach and Polk sts. Tel: (415) 556 1843.

Return the same way to Pier 39 or take the cable car from the Hyde St terminal back to the centre.

National Maritime Museum

The nearby National Maritime Museum displays model ships, photographs and nautical memorabilia. It has recently been renovated and is still undergoing some construction.
Beach and Polk sts. Tel: (415) 447 5000. www.nps.gov. Open: daily 10am–4pm.

San Francisco Maritime National Historical Park

Down the street is Hyde Street Pier, part of the National Maritime Museum. Several historic ships are anchored here.
2905 Hyde St. Tel: (415) 561 7169. www.nps.gov. Open: daily 9.30am–5.30pm (5pm in winter). Admission charge.

Shopping complexes

Ghirardelli Square is a shopping complex worthy of attention. It is the original home of Ghirardelli chocolate, which is highly regarded in the US. You can still see the antique chocolate machines, and even sample the goods. (*See also p151.*)
Ghirardelli Square, 900 N Point St. Tel: (415) 775 5500. www.ghirardellisq. com. Shops open: Mon–Thur & Sun 10am–6pm, Fri & Sat 10am–9pm. Restaurant hours vary.

Golden Gate Bridge

The Golden Gate was named by John C Frémont in 1846 after the Golden Horn of Constantinople, three years before the Gold Rush. At 2.7km (1¾ miles) long, although it is 70 years old, the bridge is still one of the longest single-span suspension bridges in the world and one of the most beautiful.

Both a cycle path and a footpath cross the bridge. The walk can get pretty cold, particularly if the fog rolls in, and remember you will have to walk back; there is no direct public transport to take you. There is a vista point at the northern end of the bridge in Marin County, and the view towards San Francisco is spectacular. Photographers may want to pass under the freeway and drive up to the Marin Headlands for the same dramatic view of the city but with the bridge in the foreground.

The Golden Gate Bridge is a toll bridge but the toll is only payable driving south into San Francisco.
www.goldengatebridge.org

Golden Gate Park

The 412 hectares (1,017 acres) of parkland that stretch all the way across the western half of San Francisco can be credited to the work of 19th-century horticulturist John McLaren, who turned these hectares of rolling sand dunes into one of the great urban parks of the world.

This is a major recreation area for the local population. There is a boating lake, a lake for model boats, rhododendron dells, a casting pond for anglers and even a buffalo paddock and a working windmill. At weekends John F Kennedy Drive, the main road through the park, is closed to vehicles and open to jugglers, roller-skaters, skateboarders and anyone else who needs open space and an enthusiastic audience. In addition to the scenic value of the area there are several major attractions.

California Academy of Sciences

The Academy of Sciences is the oldest scientific institution in the western US and has been located in Golden Gate Park since 1916. The Academy was completely rebuilt in 2008 with innovative and environmentally friendly designs by architect Renzo Piano. Exhibits of the Academy include the original aquarium, a planetarium and a natural history museum.
*Tel: (415) 379 8000. www.
calacademy.org. Open: Mon–Sat
9.30am–5pm, Sun 11am–5pm.
Admission charge.*

Conservatory of Flowers

This is the oldest building in the park and the oldest glass and wood Victorian greenhouse in North America. It was shipped over from London and erected on its present site in 1879. It is a replica of the great Palm House in London's Kew Gardens and is filled with palms and numerous other tropical plants.
*Tel: (415) 831 2090.
www.conservatoryofflowers.org.
Open: Tue–Sun 10am–4.30pm.
Admission charge (free on first
Tue of every month).*

The Japanese Tea Garden in Golden Gate Park

Grateful Dead mural, Haight-Ashbury

Japanese Tea Garden

Adjacent to the Asian Art Museum is the calm and tranquil Japanese Tea Garden, laid out in traditional Japanese style with curved bridges, waterfalls, stone lanterns and a pagoda.
Tel: (415) 752 1171.
www.japaneseteagardensf.com.
Open: daily 9am–6pm, 9am–4.45pm in winter (tea house closes 30min earlier).
Admission charge (free on Mon, Wed & Fri before 10am).

MH de Young Museum

The de Young collection covers European and American paintings up to the 1900s, period furniture, glassware, silverware, and over 600 tribal rugs from central Asia. The museum was seriously damaged in the Loma Prieta earthquake and a state-of-the-art facility opened in 2005. The striking building, designed by Herzog & de Meuron, integrates art, architecture and landscape in one multifaceted destination showcasing the museum's priceless collections. The observation tower affords wonderful views.

Tel: (415) 750 3600.
www.deyoungmuseum.org.
Open: Tue–Sun 9.30am–5.15pm, Fri until 8.45pm (tower closes 45min earlier). Closed: Mon. Admission charge (free first Tue of every month).

San Francisco Botanical Garden at Strybing Arboretum

This is a 28-hectare (70-acre) park within a park, containing over 6,000 species of bushes and trees. There is a redwood trail, moon-viewing garden and a fragrant garden for the visually impaired. All the plants are labelled, and the avid horticulturist should be able to find plenty to fully occupy a half-day visit.
Tel: (415) 661 1316.
www.sfbotanicalgarden.org.
Open: daily 9am–6pm in summer, 10am–5pm in winter.
Admission charge (free on second Tue of every month).

Haight-Ashbury

The name refers to the junction of Haight Street and Ashbury Street, which in the 1960s was to the hippies what North Beach was to the beatniks of the 1950s.

A few psychedelic relics remain. The odd 'head shop' selling drug-related items still manages to stay in business; antique clothing stores rub shoulders with gay bars and art galleries. You may even see the occasional hippy complete with beads, kaftan and sandals.

Japantown

The area bounded by Geary and Post streets and Laguna and Fillmore streets has become the Japanese equivalent of Chinatown.

Unfortunately it has none of the colour and atmosphere of its Chinese counterpart. **The Japan Center**, a 2-hectare (5-acre) commercial development that is the heart of Japantown, is an ugly modern series of buildings.

Once you enter the buildings things get better. Although the whole development is a little too bland, the shops do to some extent capture the flavour of Japan. The restaurants most certainly do. Many of the restaurants and sushi bars, both in the Japan Center and the surrounding streets, are totally authentic and serve excellent food.

The **Nihonmachi Mall** on Buchanan Street is one of the pleasant corners of Japantown. You pass under a *torii* gate to a cobblestone pathway that meanders past fountains. On either side of the mall are delightful little shops selling everything from *shoji* screens to antique kimonos. At the end of the mall, across Post Street, stands the five-tiered **Peace Pagoda** designed by the eminent Japanese architect Yoshiro Taniguchi.

Lombard Street

The Crookedest Street in the World winds down from Hyde Street to Leavenworth Street in a series of hairpin bends.

It's more fun to watch than to drive down Lombard Street yourself

There are spectacular views across to Coit Tower from the top before you plunge down the brick-paved street lined with carefully tended flowerbeds.

Marin City

A short drive, or a short ferry ride from San Francisco's Ferry Building, takes you to one of the most spectacularly situated towns in the Bay Area.

Sausalito tumbles down a hillside to an almost Mediterranean corniche, giving unparalleled views of San Francisco. This popular tourist destination has the requisite restaurants, expensive shops and art galleries.

Nob Hill

On the high point of the California Street cable-car line, Nob Hill still caters to the elite. This was where the wealthy of San Francisco built their mansions in the mid-1800s, and in 1882 Robert Louis Stevenson described it as 'the hill of palaces'.

Most of these mansions were destroyed by fire following the 1906 earthquake, but one survived. The imposing brownstone mansion of James Flood still sits at the top of the hill and it is now the private Pacific Union Club. Two of the city's grand hotels are neighbours of the Flood Mansion: the Fairmont and, across the road, the Mark Hopkins.

Grace Cathedral is at 1100 California Street at Taylor Street.

VICTORIAN HOUSES

Fine examples of Victorian architecture can be found all over San Francisco, but the view from Alamo Square with the modern city in the background has become an icon of the city. Alamo Square is on Steiner and Fulton streets and late afternoon is the best time to photograph this classic cliché.

On Franklin Street the Haas-Lilienthal House, which was built in 1886, is the only fully furnished Victorian house open to the public. The most unusual is the Octagon House on Gough Street at Union Street. This eight-sided house has been fully restored and tours are available.

Several Victorian houses have more recently been converted into bed and breakfast establishments.

North Beach

This is still a distinctively Italian neighbourhood in spite of recent encroachment by Chinatown.

In the 1950s it was the bohemian centre of San Francisco. Jack Kerouac and other Beat generation poets would congregate in the Italian coffee bars and in the City Lights Bookstore. The bookshop is still in business on the corner of Columbus Avenue across Jack Kerouac Alley from Vesuvio Cafe, another Beatnik haunt, and it remains an important cultural gathering place. Columbus Avenue is the main street through North Beach and it is crossed by Broadway, which has long had a reputation for its strip joints. A bronze plaque on the wall of the Condor commemorates the building as 'the birthplace of the world's first topless and bottomless entertainment'.

This tawdry strip of cheap sex shows is gradually changing for the better, and north of Broadway, around Washington Square, life in Little Italy continues at the steady pace it has always known. Old men sit on benches in the square conversing in Italian, and young men sit in the bars and coffee houses watching the world go by.

North Beach is a great place to relax and escape to Europe for a few hours.

Palace of Fine Arts

In 1915 the Panama–Pacific Exposition extended all the way across what is now the Marina District. Today there is only one remnant, the Palace of Fine Arts.

The building was designed by the eminent San Francisco architect Bernard Maybeck as a stucco construction, but it deteriorated so severely that in the 1960s it was completely reconstructed in concrete.

More than just a good-looking building, the Palace of Fine Arts houses an auditorium and one of the most entertaining museums in San Francisco.

The **Exploratorium** is a hands-on science museum for children of all ages. Over 600 exhibits wait to be discovered by visitors. *Scientific American* magazine deemed it to be 'the best science museum in the world'.

The Tactile Dome is one of the most popular exhibits in the museum. In this pitch-black sensory chamber, visitors have to feel their way through a maze of passages and textures in total darkness. It is so popular that reservations are required (*tel: (415) 561 0362*). *The Exploratorium, Marina Blvd & Lyon St. Tel: (415) 561 0360. www. exploratorium.edu. Open: Tue–Sun 10am–5pm. Closed: Mon. Admission charge (free on first Wed of every month).*

Restored in concrete, the Palace of Fine Arts has a grand rotunda

Walk: Downtown San Francisco

San Francisco is one of the few American cities that lends itself to walking. This walk covers the best areas of the commercial, shopping and historic areas of downtown San Francisco.

Allow 2 hours.

Start from Union Square. On the Stockton St side of the square look for Maiden Lane. This narrow street has exclusive boutiques and galleries. On the left you will see a Frank Lloyd Wright

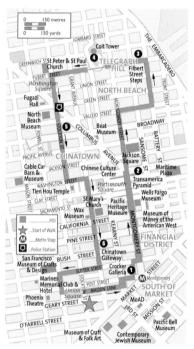

building that was a model for New York's Guggenheim Museum. Follow Maiden Lane to Kearny St, turn left, walk to Post St and turn right.

1 Crocker Galleria

This glass-domed shopping mall off Montgomery Street was modelled on the Galleria in Milan.
Go through the Galleria and turn right, then continue along the canyon of Montgomery St, the Wall Street of the West. This is the financial heart of northern California.

2 Transamerica Pyramid

The unmistakable building on the corner of Montgomery and Washington streets is the tallest structure in the city at 260m (853ft). At the present time the building has no public access or visitor facilities other than the first-floor lobby.
Continue along Montgomery St. Once out of the financial area, the street starts to climb. Continue up the increasingly

steep street and through the atmospheric Jackson Square Historical District as far as Vallejo St. There are good views of both the city and the bay. Turn right and descend to Battery St. Turn left. This is the centre of the advertising industry and all the major agencies are along here. Continue along Battery to Levi's Plaza, the home of Levi Strauss Jeans. Opposite is Filbert St.

3 Filbert Street Steps
The steps rise steeply from Battery Street straight up to Coit Tower. The steps are one of the undiscovered treasures of the city. They pass carefully tended gardens and a profusion of flowers during the summer months. It's a strenuous climb. Watch for feral parrots that are often seen here.

4 Coit Tower
The steps emerge at this distinctive landmark on top of Telegraph Hill. Inside the tower there are wonderful murals painted during the 1930s depicting the workers of San Francisco. The top of the tower gives good views of the city and the bay.
From the tower continue down Filbert St to the Italian North Beach District. Walk as far as Stockton St and turn left. The coffee and garlic aromas of North Beach will give way to smells of Chinatown.

5 Stockton Street
Always busy, Stockton Street is where the Chinese shop. This is the real Chinatown.

Continue along Stockton to Washington St. Turn left and walk one block to Grant Ave. Turn right. Grant is the tourists' Chinatown with gift shops, jewellers and restaurants.

6 Chinatown Gateway
Chinatown ends at this imposing gate, guarded by a pair of dragons.
Turn right on to Sutter St. Here are some of the most fashionable and expensive shops in San Francisco. Walk up Sutter to Powell St. Turn left on Powell and return to Union Square.

Transamerica Pyramid and the Flatiron Sentinel Building

Wine

When a Stag's Leap Wine Cellars' 1973 Cabernet Sauvignon won first place in a blind tasting in Paris, competing against the finest French wines, Californian wine had truly arrived.

The first grapevines were introduced to San Diego in 1769 by the Spanish missionaries. The vineyards extended northwards with the establishment of the missions, but it was not until the Gold Rush that winemaking came into its own. The Buena Vista Winery was founded in Sonoma in 1857 and over the next two decades European immigrants built wineries throughout Napa, Sonoma, Santa Clara and the Central Valley.

The tasting room, Sterling Vineyards, Napa Valley

The crop at Pine Ridge Winery, Yountville

The industry ground to a halt during 13 years of prohibition, and by 1933, when the law was repealed, was in complete disarray.

Techniques and vine stocks improved vastly over the ensuing years so that in the early 1970s Californian wines could compete with the best in the world.

The finest wines are produced from the white Chardonnay grape and the red Cabernet Sauvignon. However, very good wine is produced from virtually every variety of grape including Sauvignon Blanc, Pinot Noir, Chenin Blanc, Riesling, Merlot and California's very own Zinfandel – the Beaujolais of California.

The major wineries extend from Lake County and Mendocino down to the Santa Ynez Valley near Santa Barbara. Napa Valley, a one-hour drive north of San Francisco, is the heart of Californian wine country and it is here that some of the world's finest wines are produced.

Many of the wineries offer tastings and tours. Maps and leaflets are readily available, especially at local tourist offices.

Northern California

WINE COUNTRY

The wine country begins a mere one-hour drive to the north of San Francisco. Altogether four counties comprise the major wine-growing area: Napa, Sonoma, Lake and Mendocino. However, it is Napa Valley that has become synonymous with wine, and many of the finest wines in the world are produced here. The Sonoma County wines are often the equal of their Napa neighbours, and it was in the historic town of Sonoma that the Californian wine industry started in the mid-19th century.

Napa Valley

There are over 300 wineries in this valley, which is only 48km (30 miles) long and 5km (3 miles) wide.

Most wineries are concentrated along Highway 29 between Napa and Calistoga. Unfortunately, this road also has the greatest concentration of traffic. It is the main road through the valley, and during the summer and at weekends it is so busy that the cars can be bumper to bumper all the way.

To avoid this, try the Silverado Trail parallel to Highway 29 (*see p110*).

Most of the wineries offer guided tours and tastings. Several wineries require advance reservations for tours and most charge a fee for tastings.

Calistoga

At the northern end of the Napa Valley the small town of Calistoga has been an important spa since the mid-1800s.

The natural thermal activity in the area and the profusion of hot springs have resulted in a thriving business in steam baths, mud baths and massage.

Clos Pegase

This is one of the most interesting wineries, with a focus on art and mythology. The spectacular building was designed by eminent American architect Michael Graves, who was the winner of a competition held in collaboration with the San Francisco Museum of Modern Art.

The winery houses the vast art collection of Jan Schrem, the owner. Tours include the wine-ageing caves. *1060 Dunaweal Ln, Calistoga. Tel: (707) 942 4981. www.clospegase.com. Open: daily 10.30am–5pm.*

Domaine Chandon

The tour here covers the manufacture of sparkling wine at one of the valley's few champagne-type wine producers. This modern winery also has one of the area's outstanding restaurants. *1 California Dr, Yountville. Tel: (888) 242 6366. www.chandon.com. Open: daily 10am–5pm.*

Glen Ellen

The tiny village of Glen Ellen lies to the west of Sonoma on Highway 12 at the southern end of the Valley of the Moon. This sleepy corner of the wine country is notable as the former home of writer Jack London.

Healdsburg

Off Highway 101 northwest of Santa Rosa, this genteel town has some of the area's trendiest hotels, shops and restaurants. For posh picnic supplies, call in at the renowned Oakville Grocery, on the corner of the lovely main square.

The Hess Collection Winery

At the southern end of the valley, close to Napa town, the Hess Collection offers a self-guided tour of the winery and a multi-level gallery with an impressive collection of modern paintings.

4411 Redwood Rd, Napa. Tel: (707) 255 1144. www.hesscollection.com. Open: daily 10am–5.30pm.

Jack London State Historic Park

West of Glen Ellen is the 324-hectare (800-acre) Jack London State Historic Park. The land was London's beloved Beauty Ranch and within the park lie the remains of the Wolf House, destroyed by a mysterious fire before completion in 1913.

After London's death in 1916, his wife Charmian built the House with Happy Walls, now a museum dedicated to London with memorabilia of his travels, particularly in the South Pacific. The park has numerous walking trails and is ideal for picnics.
Open: daily 10am–5pm. Free admission.

Old Faithful of California

This is one of the few geysers in the world that erupts at regular intervals.

If you have never seen a geyser, the novelty value may make this attraction worth the nominal entrance fee. The rundown buildings that are an excuse for an entrance prevent the geyser

(Cont. on p112)

Oak wine barrels stacked outside Sterling Vineyards, Napa Valley

Tour: Silverado Trail

This country drive not only avoids the heavy traffic of Highway 29 through Napa Valley but passes through some of the most scenic and unspoilt sections of the California wine country. The Silverado Trail was originally a stagecoach route and even today it has a strong feeling of the past. A map is available from the Napa tourist office, as are brochures offering discounts on some tastings.

Allow 2 hours, including stops.

Travelling north, turn right off Highway 29 at Trancas St in Napa. Follow Trancas

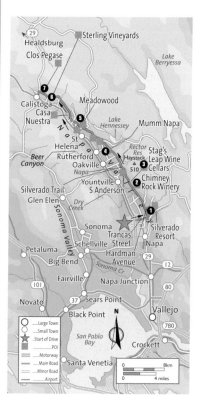

for 1.6km (1 mile) and turn left on to the Silverado Trail.

A short way along the Silverado Trail turn right on to Hardman Ave. At the end of Hardman turn right and the Silverado Resort is on the left.

1 Silverado Resort

This magnificent plantation-style building was originally the 1870 home of General John Miller. It is now one of the finest resort facilities in California, with two championship golf courses, seventeen tennis courts and two gourmet restaurants.
Return to the Silverado Trail and turn right. Drive for 3km (2 miles), passing rolling vineyards on both sides of the road.

2 Chimney Rock Winery

A golf course used to be located on this prime vineyard land. The distinctive Dutch architecture of the winery transports the visitor to the wine country of South Africa. There is a

public tasting room and tours by appointment.
5350 Silverado Trail, Napa.
Tel: (800) 257 2641.
Return to the Silverado Trail and turn right. Drive for 1.6km (1 mile).

3 Stag's Leap Wine Cellars

This is the winery that put Napa Valley on the international wine map in the 1970s, when one of its Cabernet Sauvignon wines beat the best French wines at a blind tasting in Paris.

The winery has a tasting room open to the public, and tours are available by appointment.
5766 Silverado Trail, Napa.
Tel: (707) 261 6441.
Continue north on the Silverado Trail, passing several small wineries. Mumm Napa is on the left.

4 Mumm Napa

This state-of-the-art winery, owned in part by the great French champagne house, is one of the few producers of champagne-style wines in the valley. Open for both tours and tasting.
8445 Silverado Trail, Rutherford.
Tel: (707) 967 7700.
Drive 3km (2 miles) north to Howell Mountain Rd. Turn right and then immediately left on to a winding lane.

5 Meadowood

Beautifully situated in the midst of a tree-covered valley, this exclusive retreat has a spa, golf, tennis, fine dining and a perfectly manicured croquet lawn.

900 Meadowood Ln, St Helena.
Tel: (800) 458 8080.
The Trail winds north through yet more vineyards. After 6km (4 miles), turn left on to Dunaweal Lane.

6 Sterling Vineyards

An aerial tram transports visitors to this hilltop winery. In addition to the wine, there are magnificent views down the Napa Valley (*see p112*).
1111 Dunaweal Ln, Calistoga.
Tel: (800) 726 6136.

7 Clos Pegase

Directly across the road from Sterling, the controversial architecture of this winery is hard to miss. Inside you will find a very impressive art collection.
1060 Dunaweal Ln, Calistoga.
Tel: (707) 942 4981.
Continue along the Silverado Trail to its end in Calistoga. Turn left into town.

Sterling Vineyards' aerial tramway car, Calistoga

being seen from the road. Behind these buildings is a pool of water out of which a 30m (100ft) jet shoots every 20 to 40 minutes. There is also a small petting zoo with goats, sheep and llamas.

1299 Tubbs Ln, 2.5km (1¹/2 miles) north of Calistoga off Hwy 29. Tel: (707) 942 6463. www.oldfaithfulgeyser.com. Open: winter daily 9am–5pm, summer daily 9am–6pm. Admission charge.

Robert Mondavi Winery

Robert Mondavi has been one of the great innovators in the Californian wine industry. His collaboration with Baron Rothschild of Bordeaux developed a new breed of Californian wine. The tour covers the whole process of state-of-the-art winemaking.

7801 St Helena Hwy, Oakville. Tel: (888) 766 6328. www.robertmondavi.com. Open: daily 10am–5pm.

Rubicon Estate

The magnificent Gothic Revival winery was built in 1879 and is one of the most impressive in the valley. The winery was bought by film director Francis Ford Coppola and now houses an exhibition of Hollywood memorabilia in addition to the expected winery attractions.

1991 St Helena Hwy, Rutherford. Tel: (800) 782 4266. www.rubiconestate.com. Open: daily 10am–5pm.

ROBERT LOUIS STEVENSON

Stevenson was born in Edinburgh in 1850. In 1876 he met and fell in love with a married American woman, Fanny Osborne. She returned to California in 1878 and the following year he decided to join her.

Stevenson was already suffering from severe respiratory problems when he reached California, but he managed to eke out a meagre living in Monterey and San Francisco. His walks along what is now Pebble Beach, Monterey, are thought to have provided material for his popular novel *Treasure Island*.

In 1880 Stevenson married Fanny. Their honeymoon spent near St Helena in the Napa Valley resulted in the book, *The Silverado Squatters*. He died in Samoa in 1894.

St Helena

This charming little town is the hub of Napa Valley and it still looks much the same as it did in the 1890s. This is yet another place that Robert Louis Stevenson spent a few months in 1880, and the mandatory memorabilia collection is housed in the Silverado Museum wing of the public library. It was in St Helena that he wrote notes that he incorporated into the book *The Silverado Squatters*.

Sterling Vineyards

This attractive winery has stunning views of the surrounding countryside. The admission price includes a scenic tram ride, self-guided tour, wine tastings and a souvenir wine glass.

1111 Dunaweal Ln, Calistoga. Tel: (800) 726 6136.

www.sterlingvineyards.com.
Open: daily 10.30am–5pm.

Valley of the Moon

Only a 30-minute drive west from Napa, the Valley of the Moon (often known as Sonoma Valley) extends from Sonoma to Santa Rosa. This premium winegrowing region was named by writer Jack London, who made his last home here.

Sonoma

The central plaza of Sonoma was laid out by General Vallejo in 1835 and it is surrounded by one of the finest groups of Mexican-era adobe buildings in northern California. Just off the main plaza, the San Francisco de Solano mission is the most northerly of the

chain and was the last to be built, in 1823.

Although Napa Valley now wears the winemakers' crown, it was Sonoma where the industry started. In 1857 Agoston Haraszthy built the **Buena Vista Carneros Winery** at 18000 Old Winery Road, Sonoma (*tel: (707) 265 1472; www.buenavistacarneros.com*). There are tours available and the grounds are a perfect spot for a picnic.

Buena Vista was the first commercial enterprise, but in 1825 padres from the mission had planted a huge vineyard near Fourth Street East in Sonoma. In 1904 the Sebastiani family purchased it and they have been operating the winery ever since at 389 Fourth Street East, Sonoma (*tel: (707) 933 3230; www.sebastiani.com*).

Northern California

Beauty Ranch Cottage, Jack London State Historic Park

SACRAMENTO

Rather than San Francisco or Los Angeles, Sacramento became California's capital city – and appropriately so, since the state's modern history began near here, at a site on the American River. Carpenter James Marshall, sent upstream to construct a new lumber mill by John Sutter, one of Sacramento's first settlers, also discovered gold in the millrace.

Sutter's dreams of an agricultural empire were dashed by the 1849 California Gold Rush. Almost overnight his small adobe enclave grew into a commercial centre of well over half a million people, and by 1854 Sacramento had become the state capital. Sacramento is a city at once relaxed and refreshing – except in extreme summer heat when even rose bushes wilt. Most historic sights and other attractions are easily accessible from downtown. At least one local event, the annual Jazz Jubilee held over the Memorial Day weekend, is worthy of rescheduling one's holiday.

California State Capitol

The state's golden-domed Capitol building is Sacramento's stately centrepiece, situated at 10th Street and the Capitol Mall (between L and N streets). Particularly worth seeing are the Senate and Assembly chambers.

Outside is the 16-hectare (40-acre) Capitol Park, an impressive arboretum and California's Vietnam Veterans Memorial. Free tickets for guided tours (*offered daily on the hour, 9am–4pm*) are available at the museum office in the Capitol's basement (*tel: (916) 324 0333*).
www.capitolmuseum.ca.gov. Open: daily 9am–5pm.

California State Indian Museum and Sutter's Fort

Near the Capitol, the California State Indian Museum offers a fine collection of Native American artefacts and exhibits of California's first citizens, whose cultures have been almost obliterated by subsequent history.

Adjacent Sutter's Fort, the valley's first non-native settlement, represents that history. Established in 1839, only a few sections of the original adobe walls survived the Gold Rush but the restored complex is well worth a look.
2618 K St. Tel: (916) 324 0971.
www.parks.ca.gov.
Sutter's Fort: 2701 L St.
Tel: (916) 445 4422. www.parks.ca.gov.
Museums open: daily 10am–5pm.
Admission charge.

Crocker Art Museum

This museum is itself a work of art, in the high Italianate Victorian style. The Crocker is also one of the oldest public art museums in the west, noted for its Californian art and photography.
216 O St. Tel: (916) 264 5423.
www.crockerartmuseum.org.
Open: Tue & Wed 10am–7pm, Fri–Sun 10am–5pm, Thur 10am–9pm. Closed: Mon. Admission charge.

Governor's Mansion

Peculiar to California, and due to pugnacious state politics, is the fact that there is no official governor's residence – not since 1967 when then-Governor Ronald Reagan fled this fine Victorian house and it became a public museum.
1526 H St. Tel: (916) 323 3047. www.parks.ca.gov. Open: daily 10am–4pm for guided tours only. Admission charge.

Old Sacramento

At the west end of J Street, Old Sacramento is a colourful 'city' of refurbished buildings of the Gold Rush era and a state historic park in its entirety. Many of the shops re-create Sacramento's frontier past as well as the superb museums. The **California State Railroad Museum** at 125 I Street (*tel: (916) 445 6645; www.csrmf.com*) has an exceptional collection of restored locomotives and old railroad cars.

Also worthwhile in Old Sacramento is the **Sacramento History Museum** at 101 I Street (*tel: (916) 808 7059; www.historicoldsac.org*), which has exhibits about the Gold Rush.

Self-guided walking tours take in the highlights of the area; pick up a leaflet at the **Old Sacramento Visitor Center** (*1002 Second St; tel: (916) 442 7644; www.oldsacramento.com*), which also has details about local events.

The stretch of the river bordering Old Sacramento is attractive, and you can spend the night on the *Delta King* riverboat, which is moored at 1000 Front Street (*tel: (916) 444 5464; www.deltaking.com*).

To the northeast is the former McClellan Air Force Base, which is now home to the **Aerospace Museum of California** (*3200 Freedom Park Dr, McClellan; tel: (916) 643 3192; www.aerospacemuseumofcalifornia.org; open: Tue–Sat 9am–5pm, Sun 10am–5pm*).

Sacramento's Capitol building

GOLD COUNTRY

Just as Nevada is known as the Silver State, it is no accident that California became the Golden State. The 1849 California Gold Rush created modern-day California. And the Gold Rush began here, when James Marshall made the first gold discovery, on the western slope of the Sierra Nevada along the 483km (300-mile) stretch of small towns and rolling foothills now loosely connected by Highway 49.

The Spanish myth of *la veta madre* or 'the mother lode' refers to a single rich vein of ore once considered the source of all gold in the territory. Historical purists will point out that the mother lode actually refers only to the territory's southern mines: those from Placerville south. The northern mines, not included under this interpretation of the mother lode, include the areas of Auburn, Grass Valley and Nevada City, as well as the wild and woolly Yuba and Feather River watersheds reaching all the way up to Oroville north of Sacramento.

California's Gold Country is ideal for one-day and weekend excursions, but it also warrants much slower exploration. The area offers a number of low-key attractions that include historical museums and parks, boutique wineries and produce stands. For those looking for a quieter getaway there are hiking and cycling treks in some quite outstanding countryside, as well as gold panning, fishing and (in non-drought years) superb white-water rafting.

The northern mines

Auburn and Coloma

Partly included within the 97-hectare (240-acre) **Marshall Gold Discovery State Historic Park** (*tel: (530) 622 3470*) 16km (10 miles) south of Auburn, Coloma marks the spot where James Marshall found gold in early 1848. This birthplace of the state's Gold Rush, now a mecca for white-water rafters on the American River's south fork, includes a replica of **Sutter's Mill**, restored historic buildings, an excellent museum, and commercial shops and galleries (*www.parks.ca.gov; open: daily 10am–4pm*).

The community of Auburn, just north, is noted for its historic Old Town and the Placer County Courthouse, built entirely of local materials and beautifully restored. Worth more time, though, is the **Bernhard Museum Complex** (*tel: (530) 889 6500*), which is completely furnished with Victorian antiques.

Grass Valley

North of Auburn are the twin foothill towns of **Grass Valley** and **Nevada City**, popular getaways for Californians. Once home to notorious dancer Lola Montez, who scandalised Europe (and eventually even San Francisco), Grass Valley was also the home town of Montez's protégée Lotta Crabtree, darling of the gold camps, and America's first millionaire entertainer.

Empire Mine State Historic Park at 10791 East Empire Street (*tel: (530) 273 8522; open: daily winter 10am–5pm,* summer 10am–6pm) is a huge indoor-outdoor museum of mine shafts and ruins, opulent buildings, gracious gardens and interpretive walks and displays. The Empire Mine was one of the richest and oldest hard rock mines in the state when it closed in 1956. Here, you can see the family cottage of its owner William Bourn.

Nevada City

Historically, Nevada City has been host to innovators and innovations. World-class soprano Emma Nevada and Andrew Hallidie, inventor of the cable car, were both born here.

Nevada City created new and radical mining techniques, including hydraulic mining. Social engineering was also no surprise: US Senator A J Sargent, a local resident, prepared legislation that led to American women's suffrage. Meetings held here ultimately established both the University of California and Pacific Gas & Electric, the world's largest utility company.

Noted today for its fine Victorian homes, active arts community and the historic **National Hotel**, Nevada City's most unusual legacy is actually outside town and quite remote. **Malakoff Diggins State Historic Park** (tel: (530) 265 2740; www.parks.ca.gov) is an oddly enchanting environmental horror, including a massive mine pit with colourful crags and spires created in the 1870s by the hugely destructive method of hydraulic mining.

Beyond Malakoff Diggins, Highway 49 weaves through rugged Yuba River Canyon past the striking tin-roofed towns of **Downieville** and **Sierra City**, birthplace of the eccentric Gold Rush fraternity of E Clampus Vitus. (The Clampers' ancient motto, 'I believe because it is absurd', speaks truth even in modern-day California.)

Beyond Sierra City is the **Gold Lakes** region and **Plumas-Eureka State Park** (tel: (530) 836 2380; www.parks.ca.gov).

The southern mines
Placerville to Jackson

South of Coloma is **Placerville** (once known as Hangtown, owing to the local enthusiasm for gallows justice). These days Placerville is primarily proud of its 24-hectare (60-acre) **Gold Bug Park and Mine** (tel: (530) 642 5207; www.goldbugpark.org), America's only city-owned gold mine.

First known as Pokerville, then Puckerville, these days **Plymouth** offers few pleasures except fine regional wineries, including the **Sobon Estate** (tel: (209) 245 4455; www.sobonwine.com; tastings daily 9.30am–5pm) northeast of town on Shenandoah Road, and a state historic landmark.

The next stop south is **Drytown**, once cherished by miners for its 27 saloons. **Jackson** is well worth several hours of exploration, with a side trip east up Highway 88 to both **Indian Grinding Rock State Park** and the serene Gold Rush town of **Volcano**.

Gold

When James Marshall discovered gold in the millrace of a sawmill in Coloma in 1848, the course of Californian history changed dramatically. Within a year, thousands of fortune seekers headed west and started the migration that continues even today.

Gold had always been the carrot dangling in front of the explorers of this frontier land, and once its discovery had been made towns mushroomed overnight.

The legacy of this period still survives in the string of towns along

Living history character William McIntosh pans for gold at Columbia Diggins, Columbia State Historic Park

Panning equipment in Woods Creek, Jamestown

Highway 49 from Nevada City down to Mariposa.

'Weekend miners' still go panning in the rivers, and some commercial mines have reopened. It is thought that as much gold as has already been mined is still in the Californian ground.

Mine tours are given at the old Empire Mine in Grass Valley, and the North Star Mine has a museum with a vast display of mining equipment.

In the **Malakoff Diggins State Historic Park**, 26km (16 miles) north of Nevada City, you can see an impressive example of landscape erosion as a result of hydraulic mining.

A replica of Sutter's Mill, where gold was discovered, has been constructed on the original site in Coloma. Gold pans are available to rent for anyone wanting to attempt a re-creation of the historic event.

Many shops have California gold for sale and there is no shortage of museum exhibits. Perhaps the most impressive display of the immense wealth extracted from the California soil is the $5 million pyramid of gold bars on display at the Old Mint in San Francisco (see map p85).

Victorian building in Nevada City

Angels Camp

Past Mokelumne Hill and San Andreas is the little city of Angels Camp, made famous by Mark Twain's first successful story, *The Celebrated Jumping Frog of Calaveras County*. The roads here were surfaced in 1928, the same year the community launched its annual Jumping Frog Jubilee (real frogs, rentals available), held in May.

Heading east on Highway 4 is **Murphys**, with its odd **Old Timers' Museum** and the fine **Murphys Historic Hotel** (genuine bullet holes in the doors, wonderful western bar). Nearby are **Mercer Caverns** and **Moaning Cavern** (*see p147*). Up the highway is **Calaveras Big Trees State Park** (*tel: (209) 795 2334; www.parks.ca.gov*), a few rare groves of Giant Sequoia.

Columbia and Sonora

Columbia, the 'Gem of the Southern Mines' 16km (10 miles) south of Angels

Camp, is a must-do destination for aficionados of American Westerns. Quite a few, including *High Noon*, were filmed here. The town's authenticity is painstakingly preserved; **Columbia State Historic Park** (*tel: (209) 588 9128; www.parks.ca.gov*) offers entire city blocks of oddities in addition to museums, an exquisite period hotel, saloons, stagecoach rides, and events such as the annual Firemen's Muster in May and the Columbia Diggins living history weekend in late May/early June. Columbia is a real town, and most shops and restaurants are open 10am–5pm (or later) every day.

The adjacent working town of **Sonora** has its own claims to fame, including historic buildings, fine inns and decent restaurants.

Jamestown

Just south is Jamestown or 'Jimtown', another picturesque city popular with Western film-makers. Downtown features the opportunity to practise panning for gold in the horse trough outside the livery stable on Main Street (free for children only). Adults can also hunt for riches with Miner John from **Jamestown Gold Panning** (*tel: (209) 984 4038; www.jamestowngold panning.com*). Also fun for families is **Railtown 1897 State Historic Park** (*tel: (203) 984 3953; www.railtown1897. com*). This 9-hectare (23-acre) park offers picnic grounds and an open-air collection of old railroad cars, plus various steam-powered train tours.

Coulterville

Some 32km (20 miles) south is
Coulterville, a refreshing rural
community almost unperturbed by
progress. A state historic landmark in
its entirety, Coulterville offers blocks
of Gold Rush period buildings, an
eight-tonne steam engine and a
hanging tree.

Worth an indoor stroll is
Coulterville's **Northern Mariposa
County History Center** (*tel: (209) 878
3015*), a crumbling stone museum
complete with rifles, gold scales, and
Victorian memorabilia from *High
Noon*. Across the highway is the **Hotel
Jeffery** and adjacent **Magnolia Saloon**,
with swing doors and musty artefacts
and photos.

Bear Valley to Mariposa

From Coulterville, take the back-roads
route into Yosemite National Park or
dive down into Merced River Canyon
on the loneliest stretch of Highway 49.
The latter passes what remains of **Bear
Valley**, one-time HQ for the mining
empire of explorer John C Frémont.
Southernmost of the major gold camps
is **Mariposa**. Just off Highway 140 at
Jessie and 12th streets is the excellent
Mariposa Museum and History Center
(*tel: (209) 966 2924*). The county
courthouse on Bullion Street features a
good mineral collection. But the local
crown jewels are at the **California State
Mining and Mineral Museum** with
samples of the state's mineral wealth
(*tel: (209) 742 7625; www.parks.ca.gov*).

LAKE TAHOE AND ENVIRONS

'The fairest picture the whole earth
affords', according to Mark Twain. Lake
Tahoe in the Sierra Nevada is North
America's largest alpine lake: 35km
(22 miles) long and 19km (12 miles)
across, with a 116km (72-mile)
shoreline. But its size is not its biggest
attraction. Its beauty is partially due to
the incredible clarity of the cold lake
water, almost as pure as distilled water.
Peculiar is the fact that Lake Tahoe
never freezes, due to the lake's great
depth. Beloved by Californians, Tahoe's
shoreline is largely privately owned.

Travellers, however, can enjoy the
lake itself at popular public parks. The
Tahoe area also offers some of the finest
skiing in North America and trails into
several spectacular Sierra Nevada
wilderness areas. Near Tahoe are other
fascinations, including the tiny town of
Truckee, where Charlie Chaplin filmed
The Gold Rush. Since Lake Tahoe

SOUTHERN MINES MISCELLANY

For more information, contact:
Amador County Chamber of Commerce
571 Hwy 49, Jackson, CA 95642.
Tel: (209) 223 0350.
www.amadorcountychamber.com
Calaveras County Visitors Bureau
1192 S Main St, Angels Camp, CA 95222.
Tel: (800) 225 3764. www.gocalaveras.com
El Dorado County Chamber of Commerce
542 Main St, Placerville, CA 95667.
Tel: (530) 621 5885. www.eldoradocounty.org
Tuolumne County Visitors Bureau
542 W Stockton Rd, Sonora, CA 95370.
Tel: (209) 533 4420. www.tcvb.com

straddles the California–Nevada border, the glitter of Nevada's gambling casinos, particularly at Reno and Carson City, the Nevada state capital, is also an attraction.

Tahoe area parks

Near Truckee, just off I-80 north of Tahoe, is **Donner Memorial State Park** (*tel: (530) 582 7892; www.parks.ca.gov*), where an excellent museum and various artefacts tell the grisly tale of California's notorious Donner Party. A wagon train was trapped here in 1846–7 by winter snows, and the pioneer survivors were eventually reduced to cannibalism.

North of Tahoe City on Highway 28, **Burton Creek State Park** (*tel: (530) 525 7232; www.parks.ca.gov*) is good for forest hikes. In **Tahoe City** on West Lake Boulevard is **Gatekeeper's Museum State Park** (*tel: (530) 583 1762*), several hectares with picnic areas surrounding a museum emphasising the area's native cultures and natural history.

The centrepiece of **Sugar Pine Point State Park** south of Tahoe City is the 1903 **Hellman-Ehrman Mansion**, an elegant fortress built of fine wood and stone that was part of San Francisco banker Isaias W Hellman's summer estate. The rocky lakeshore offers sunbathing and strolling. The park is also popular for picnicking and short treks (*for park and mansion: tel: (530) 525 7982; www.parks.ca.gov*).

Contiguous **DL Bliss** and **Emerald Bay State Parks** further south are

popular for camping, hiking, swimming, sunbathing and boating. It is an ambitious shoreline trek from the beaches at DL Bliss to Emerald Bay. Shorter (at least on the way down) and well worth the effort is the 1.6km (1-mile) Emerald Bay hike to **Vikingsholm** (*tel: (530) 541 3030*), a massive Scandinavian summer home built in the late 1920s at a cost of half a million dollars (tours are offered in summer). Another way to get to Vikingsholm and its fjord-like bay is by boat – a very big boat, a sternwheeler, with tours departing from **South Lake Tahoe** (*tel: (888) 867 6394*); dance cruises are also available.

Near the south shore beaches and Camp Richardson is the **Tallac Historic Site** (*tel: (530) 541 5227; www.fs.fed.us*). Here 19 historic summer homes (some fully restored) testify to Tahoe's past as the playground for California's rich and powerful. Exhibits in the **Tallac Museum** (inside 'Lucky' Baldwin's

TAHOE AREA MISCELLANY

For more information about the Tahoe area, contact:
Lake Tahoe Visitors Authority
3066 Lake Tahoe Blvd, South Lake Tahoe, CA 96150. Tel: (530) 544 5050.
www.tahoesouth.com
North Lake Tahoe Visitors and Convention Bureau
PO Box 1757, Tahoe City, CA 96145. Tel: (800) 462 5196 for written info.
www.gotahoenorth.com
Tahoe City Visitors' Information Center
380 N Lake Blvd, Tahoe City, CA 96145. Tel: (530) 581 6900.

Baldwin Estate) tell the story, or take a guided tour (summer only). Special events here include the summer Valhalla arts and music festival.

Lake Tahoe was 'discovered' internationally when the 1960 Winter Olympics were held at **Squaw Valley USA**. Skiers and non-skiers alike still make the pilgrimage to Squaw Valley, even in the summer, just to take the cable car for some breathtaking high-altitude views.

Tahoe has many other skiing areas, one of the most famous being Kirkwood to the south. Another popular activity is biking or hiking the Tahoe Rim Trail; it stretches 240km (150 miles), but you don't have to do the whole lot! A more relaxing day out can be had by heading to Sand Harbor, just south of Incline Village on Highway 28, where you'll find one of Tahoe's nicest beaches.

SOUTH FROM TAHOE

Highway 89 south from Tahoe leads into California's own big sky country, virtually inaccessible in winter except for highways serving major ski areas. Every highway pass across the Sierra Nevada has its attractions: wilderness access for backpacking, mountain lakes and rivers, family campsites, isolated ski resorts and odd old hotels and lodges, vast dark forests and aspens fiery with autumn colour.

The busy Highway 50 route to the valley over **Echo Pass** features some fine scenery, as does the one-time Pony Express route (Highway 88) west over

Spectacular scenery at Lake Tahoe

Northern California

Carson Pass and Highway 4 over **Ebbetts Pass**. Thrilling, however, is **Sonora Pass**: Highway 108 climbs to the summit in a single-lane switchback like a goat path, then suddenly slides down the other side (no trailers or recreational vehicles).

Still more spectacular is Highway 395 along the eastern slope of the **Sierra Nevada**, reached from Tahoe via Highway 89. Along the way is minuscule **Markleeville** and its unusual Cutthroat Saloon. Just west of town is the worthwhile **Grover Hot Springs State Park** (*tel: (530) 694 2248*), quite popular for its public hot and cold spring-fed pools. The opening times change frequently, so it's best to call ahead before making a special trip.

Bodie

The one-time gold-mining boom town of Bodie is California's largest ghost town, an evocative and ramshackle collection of woodframe buildings now protected as a state historic park. North of Mono Lake and reached via Highways 395 and 270 (Bodie Road), Bodie is a must-see destination. What remains of what was once one of the wildest mining camps in the west (famous for its wicked citizens, worse weather, wide streets and bad whiskey) offers absolutely non-commercial witness to the desolation of frontier life. Preserved in a state of 'arrested decay', Bodie self-guided walking tours allow visitors to peer into the weathered homes, saloons, stores,

restaurants and livery stables that populate this half-day's exploration.

Bring water and a picnic lunch because there are no services available here. The town is 'open' 8am–6pm in summer, 8am–5pm in October, 10am–3pm in winter (only the truly intrepid try to visit Bodie when the town is buried under winter snowdrifts).
Tel: (760) 647 6445. www.parks.ca.gov

Mammoth Lakes

Noted primarily as a resort centre popular with southern California skiers, the Mammoth Lakes area also offers a respite from eastern Sierra Nevada sagebrush in the form of forests, hot springs and geological oddities along area trails. Most famous here is Devil's Postpile, a fascinating collection of vertical basalt columns formed by slow-cooling lava flows. Not far from Devil's Postpile is Rainbow Falls, one of the most beautiful waterfalls in the Sierra. Traffic isn't allowed in these areas during the peak tourist summer months, so visitors must take a shuttle bus to the ranger station, then walk (it's a 6km/ 4-mile round trip to Rainbow Falls). The visitor centre is located on Highway 203 (*tel: (760) 934 2712; www.visitmammoth.com*).

Mono Lake

Once known as the Dead Sea of California, million-year-old Mono Lake is a large alkaline inland sea on the high plateau east of Yosemite. Far from 'dead', however, Mono Lake is home during at least part of each year to over 300 bird species, including almost the entire breeding population of California gulls. The saline waters here make even the worst of swimmers almost unsinkable.

Most striking, though, are Mono Lake's vast, surrounding salt flats and unusual formation of tufa – freeform pillars of calcium carbonate (limestone) originally created underwater where calcium-rich fresh spring water flowed into the salty lake. These 200- to 900-year-old bone-white spires are now exposed to view, due to Los Angeles's thirst for new water sources. Since 1941, when Mono Lake's feeder streams were first tapped, the lake level has dropped more than 14m (45ft).

The best place to explore Mono Lake's tufa collection is the South Tufa Area off Highway 120. Nearby are some interesting volcanic formations including Mono Craters, Panum Crater and Devil's Punchbowl. For more information, contact the Mono Lake Committee's information centre in Lee Vining (*tel: (760) 647 6595; www.monolake.org*).

NORTH FROM TAHOE
Lassen Volcanic National Park

Known to Native Americans as Fire Mountain, Broken Mountain and Mountain-Ripped-Apart, Lassen Peak is the southernmost volcano of the Pacific northwest's vast Cascade Range. Just over an hour's drive east of the valley towns of Chico, Red Bluff or Redding, Lassen Peak today is within a huge caldera formed by the collapse of its mother mountain (Mount Tehama) 30,000 years ago. Lassen is most famous, however, for its much more

Tufa pillars in Mono Lake

recent behaviour: surprise volcanic eruptions, culminating in a dramatic 1915 blast of steam and smoke that tossed five-tonne boulders into the sky. Lassen's theatrics created such a thrill that this pugnacious peak and its breathtaking setting were protected as a national park in 1916.

Lassen attractions and treks

Unusual at Lassen is its easy access, at least during the few short months when the main road traversing the park (Highway 89) is not blocked by snow. Many of Lassen's features are easily reached from the road, so families with small children and people with physical limitations can enjoy the wilderness.

Some treks can be quite challenging, including the steep, well-graded switchback trail to **Lassen Peak** (start early in the morning; take water and a sweater) and equally impressive **Brokeoff Mountain**. Some visitors try the park's 31km (19-mile) stretch of the **Pacific Crest Trail**. But for the truly intrepid backpacker, 75 per cent of this 42,897-hectare (106,000-acre) park is preserved as wilderness.

Other Lassen activities

Lassen Park is a volcanic wonderland, featuring three of the world's four types of volcano in addition to oddities such as boiling lakes, mudpots and sulphurous steam plumes. The best place to appreciate Lassen's fiery modern-day presence, not to mention summer wild flowers

along the way, is at **Bumpass Hell**, where the careless Mr Bumpass lost one of his legs to a boiling mudpot. (Such dangers still exist, so take all warning signs seriously.) Other fairly easy treks include **Kings Creek Falls**.

During Lassen's regular 'season', usually from mid-June until October, park rangers offer free campfire talks as well as guided treks. In winter, snowshoe hikes and cross-country ski tours are offered. (For more information, *tel: (530) 595 4480* or visit *www.nps.gov*)

Mount Shasta

Shasta is California's mountain masterpiece, the state's fifth-highest peak but more majestic than any other. Lassen's silent sister volcano, about an hour's drive north of Redding via I-5, Shasta stands alone, looming above the ancient lava landscapes and forests. Mount Shasta was one of Sierra Club founder John Muir's favourite places; he first climbed the peak in 1874. Indeed, the mountain's history is mostly one of mountaineering conquest, a feat possible today for any sensible person in reasonably good physical condition.

On an average summer day, 100 or more people attempt the ascent to the summit; about half succeed. (Climbers must register with the Forest Service office in Mount Shasta City before and after the day's efforts.) There are few trails on the mountain, but other treks are enticing. And if Shasta's wilderness areas are too crowded, **Castle Crags State Park**, about 32km (20 miles) south, is usually sublime.

Mount Shasta City at the base of the mountain offers basic services, motels and restaurants. For information about the mountain and town, contact: **Mount Shasta Chamber of Commerce and Visitors' Bureau**, *300 Pine St, Mt Shasta, CA 96067. Tel: (800) 926 4865. www.mtshastachamber.com*

Halfway between Mount Shasta and Lassen Park via Highway 89 is **McArthur–Burney Falls Memorial State Park**. Teddy Roosevelt extravagantly called Burney Falls 'the Eighth Wonder of the World'. Nearby is very remote **Ahjumawi Lava Springs State Park**, which can only be reached by boat and is home to numerous nesting waterfowl and bald eagles. (For information on both, *tel: (530) 335 2777* or go to *www.parks.ca.gov*)

THE HIGH SIERRA

The Sierra Nevada is California's most impressive natural feature. This massive granite mountain range is approximately 724km (450 miles) long, starting in the north near Mount Lassen and ending in the desert near the Tehachapi Mountains, and 97–129km (60–80 miles) wide. Some 200 million years old, it was created by volcanic activity. The dramatic peaks and valleys of the Sierra Nevada, however, were jolted into position by earthquake faulting, and then sculpted and scoured smooth by relentless glaciers during the last million years.

(*Cont. on p130*)

Northern California

Early winter dawn in the High Sierra

Trees

'General Sherman' is the largest living thing on earth. He weighs 1,407 tonnes (1,385 tons), measures 31m (103ft) around, 84m (276ft) tall and is about 2,200 years old.

'General Sherman' is a Giant Sequoia. Sequoia National Park in the Sierra Nevada mountains is home to the big trees. The massive conifers that lived when dinosaurs roamed the earth only grow at high altitudes in the mountains of California. Apart from Sequoia, small groves can be seen in Yosemite National Park at Mariposa Grove and Tuolumne Grove and at Calaveras Big Trees State Park in the Gold Country.

Coastal redwoods along the Avenue of the Giants, Northern California

By some botanical quirk, California is home for not only the biggest trees in the world but also the oldest and the tallest.

From Monterey to the Oregon border, giant redwoods live in a 48km (30-mile)-wide coastal fog belt. The tallest specimens, reaching heights of over 107m (350ft) and ages of up to 2,000 years, live in the far north near Eureka in Redwood National Park.

Groves of redwoods are never too far away on the northern California coast, and an impressive group of trees lives within a 32km (20-mile) drive of San Francisco across the Golden Gate Bridge in Muir Woods near Mill Valley. The oldest trees are not much to look at and they grow in an inaccessible, hostile environment above 3,048m (10,000ft) in the White Mountains to the east of Big Pine on Highway 395 (see p75).

The road climbs up to a barren, windswept, rocky landscape scattered with gnarled old trees that were growing when the Pyramids were being built in Egypt.

In the Schulman Grove of the Bristlecone Pine Forest, trees have been found that are over 4,600 years old.

Coastal redwoods in Navarro State Park

Technically, the High Sierra refers to the 241km (150-mile)-long portion of peaks, highlands and icy lakes above the tree line from north of Yosemite Valley south to Cottonwood Pass. In everyday usage, however, the term tends to include the entire range except the almost-urbanised areas of Lake Tahoe, and Yosemite Valley. However the High Sierra is defined, its elegant elevations are most easily appreciated from the range's steep eastern ascent. Mount

Yosemite Falls and Yosemite Meadow

Whitney near Lone Pine (*see p75*), surrounded by similarly sized sister peaks, is the tallest contiguous mountain range in the US (outside Alaska), reaching to 4,421m (14,505ft) above sea level.

Yosemite

The High Sierra's crowning glory is without doubt glacier-scoured Yosemite National Park. The park was created in 1890 over an area of 3,017sq km (1,165sq miles) that includes the finest valley and high mountain scenery in the US, wildly picturesque with almost vertical walls of granite. Its popularity is confirmed by over three million tourists who visit the park every year.

The heart and soul of the park is the Yosemite Valley. This 11km (7-mile)-long, 1.6km (1-mile)-wide canyon attracts over 80 per cent of all visiting traffic, and in the summer it can be a nightmare. During peak holiday periods every single room and campsite is booked not only in the park but also in the surrounding town, and traffic can be bumper-to-bumper. Reservations are an absolute necessity at these times, and the earlier the better. Campsites, in particular, book up well in advance.

Most people enter Yosemite National Park on Highway 140 from Merced. This is both the shortest and fastest route from I-5 and the San Francisco Bay area. A more dramatic approach is by Highway 120, which becomes the **Tioga Pass** and, at 3,031m (9,945ft), is

the highest vehicle pass in California. Most years snow closes the pass from mid-October to early May.

Whichever way you enter Yosemite, you will eventually want to make your way to the valley. Few places in the world have such a concentration of natural spectacles. Sheer rock walls rise either side of the Merced River almost as soon as you enter the valley proper. Rising 914m (3,000ft) above the valley floor, the giant granite bastion of **El Capitan** is reputedly the biggest monolith on earth. As you drive below this massive rock face it is almost impossible to gauge the scale until the insect-like climbers come into view.

Several more imposing towers of rock loom above the 27km (17-mile) loop road through the valley, including **Sentinel Dome**. The climax of the valley is the distinctive silhouette of **Half Dome**, which is the symbol of the Yosemite Park.

Northern California

Here in the core of the valley is North America's highest waterfall. The **Yosemite Falls**, near the Valley Visitor Center, cascade 739m (2,425ft) to join the Merced River. Yosemite's other main waterfall is the beautiful **Bridalveil Fall**, not far from El Capitan.

In the midst of all this incomparable wilderness is a surprisingly extensive development of accommodation, shops and restaurants. Immediately below Yosemite Falls lies **Yosemite Village**. This is always the busiest place in the whole of Yosemite; the **Valley Visitor Center** (*tel: (209) 372 0200*) is here, where wilderness permits can be obtained for overnight camping trips, although you should apply well in advance if you plan on visiting during the summer. Visit *www.nps.gov*. Some permits are available on the day. The area is a hikers' paradise and the centre has a good selection of books and maps.

Yosemite also offers guided bus and tram tours, cycling, fishing, horse riding and rock climbing. Lots of information is available at the visitor centre and at *www.nps.gov*. Another useful website is *www.yosemitepark.com*

For something less strenuous, visit the **Ansel Adams Gallery** (*tel: (209) 372 4413; www.anseladams.com*), which features work by the photographer. Several places in the park give spectacular views. The classic vista is from **Tunnel View** on the road to the awe-inspiring **Mariposa Grove** of Giant Sequoia trees. The road past **Badger Pass**, California's oldest ski resort, leads to **Glacier Point**, which, at 2,199m (7,214ft), also has stunning views.

The Tioga Pass Road crosses some of the most beautiful, unspoilt wilderness in the state. **Tenaya Lake** sits at 2,484m (8,149ft), surrounded by huge granite domes. The road opens out into **Tuolumne Meadows** before rising to the 3,030m (9,941ft) Tioga Pass.

Note that black bears frequently break into cars in order to steal food in Yosemite, and it is therefore very important you use the bear-resistant storage facilities provided.

THE NORTH COAST

Zigzagging north to the Oregon border from San Francisco's Golden Gate, the remote north coast is perhaps California's greatest treasure. Rolling headlands are common close to San Francisco. But further north the shoreline becomes rugged and rocky, in

WINTER RECREATION

Not famous as a ski resort, Lassen National Forest (which includes Lassen Volcanic National Park) still offers both challenging and family-friendly Nordic trails and ranger-guided snowshoe hikes.

For more information, contact park headquarters at **Lassen National Forest** *Tel: (530) 257 2151, or the visitor centre on (530) 335 7517.*

For Mount Shasta winter sports information, contact:
Mount Shasta Ski Park
104 Siskiyou Ave, Mt Shasta, CA 96067. Tel: (530) 926 8610. www.skipark.com

stark contrast to gentle coastal foothills, and there are great foggy strands of rare coastal redwoods, the tallest trees on earth, along with varied wildlife.

Golden Gate National Recreation Area

Though the Golden Gate Bridge and a small coastal strip in San Francisco is included, Golden Gate National Recreation Area (GGNRA) primarily includes the **Marin Headlands** and vast open spaces stretching north to Olema, bordering Point Reyes. Dramatic sea cliffs, rolling hills and protected ocean-facing valleys are temptations for serious trekkers.

GGNRA also includes the **Point Bonita Lighthouse**, several former US military installations, the **Marine Mammal Center** (a volunteer-staffed marine wildlife hospital), and beaches such as Stinson and Bolinas. Quite unique and endlessly popular for tours is **Alcatraz Island**, one of America's most infamous prisons (*see p86*).
For more information, contact Golden Gate National Recreation Area, Building 201, Fort Mason, San Francisco, CA 94123. Tel: (415) 561 4700. www.nps.gov

West Marin parks

Surrounded by the vast expanse of the Golden Gate National Recreation Area are other public and private parks, most of these easily reached from Highway 1. Well known for its fine mountaintop views is **Mount Tamalpais State Park**, which includes **Muir Woods** – an unmissable destination for redwood sightseers.

Steam vents in Lassen Volcanic National Park

North of Stinson Beach near serene Bolinas Lagoon is **Audubon Canyon Ranch**, a safe haven for many bird species and a rookery for egrets and herons (nesting sites are visible during the March–July nesting season). East of Point Reyes via Sir Francis Drake Boulevard is **Samuel P Taylor State Park**, with its redwoods and mixed forests, extensive trails and a surfaced cycle path. Scattered in sections north of Point Reyes Station and Inverness is **Tomales Bay State Park**, with its sunny and protected inland beaches.

Point Reyes National Seashore

Popular in winter for whale-watching, these 26,305 hectares (65,000 acres) of dazzling beaches, coastal dunes, lagoons, marshes and hilltop forests at Point Reyes National Seashore in Marin County are perfect for outdoor excursions at almost any time of year. Hiking trails extend in all directions; short trails from the **Bear Valley Visitor Center** lead to the US Park Service's **Morgan Horse Ranch** and **Kule Loklo**, a re-creation of a typical local Native American community.

The truly imaginative might seek evidence of privateer Sir Francis Drake, after whom the estuary here is named. Historians agree that Drake came ashore to refit his ship, the *Golden Hind*, at 'a fit and convenient harbour' somewhere on the coast of California in June 1579. People still search for signs of Drake's treasure, which some believe he jettisoned.

It is a short but many-stepped trip down to the **Point Reyes Lighthouse**, known for its astounding views. On a clear day (when the fog lifts), look due south to see the Farallon Islands, a UNESCO Biosphere Reserve with the largest variety of seabirds south of Alaska. The lighthouse has a visitor centre that offers talks and guided walks.

Also of interest is the **Point Reyes Bird Observatory** (*tel: (415) 868 0655*), established in 1965 as the first such facility in the US. The park has a total of three visitor centres that all offer information, including schedules of classes and field seminars (*1 Bear Valley Road, Point Reyes Station, CA 94956; tel: (415) 464 5100; www.nps.gov*).

The Sonoma coast

'Spectacular' is the word for the Highway 1 tour of the Sonoma County

---

MORE ON MARIN PARKS

For smaller parks in the area contact:
Muir Woods National Monument
Mill Valley, CA 94941. Tel: (415) 388 2596. www.nps.gov
Mount Tamalpais State Park
801 Panoramic Hwy, Mill Valley, CA 94941. Tel: (415) 388 2070. www.parks.ca.gov
Audubon Canyon Ranch
4900 Shoreline Hwy 1, Stinson Beach, CA 94970. Tel: (415) 868 9244. www.egret.org
Samuel P Taylor State Park
PO Box 251, Lagunitas, CA 94938. Tel: (415) 488 9897. www.parks.ca.gov
Tomales Bay State Park
1208 Pierce Point Rd, Inverness, CA 94937. Tel: (415) 669 1140. www.parks.ca.gov

coast. Apparently Alfred Hitchcock agreed, since he chose the coastal village of Bodega Bay as the location for *The Birds*. Aside from spotting Hitchcock settings, today the area is popular for beachcombing, whale-watching and eating seafood (including local Dungeness crab).

From Bodega Bay north to Jenner are the collected **Sonoma Coast State Beaches**, where the dark and dramatic face of the coast starts to show itself. (Most of the area is not recommended for swimming, and caution is advisable even for tame activities like tide-pool exploration. Offshore eddies, undertows, rip tides and rogue waves are common.) North of Jenner and the Russian River is reconstructed **Fort Ross State Historic Park** (*tel: (707) 847 3286; www.parks.ca.gov; open: daily sunrise–sunset*), established in 1812 as imperial Russia's most distant outpost. Further north, **Salt Point State Park** and **Kruse Rhododendron State Natural Reserve** (for both *tel: (707) 847 3221; www.parks.ca.gov*) offer more natural attractions in any season (particularly during peak bloom in April or May).

Northern California

North Coast beach at Point Reyes National Seashore

Northern California

Mendocino, Fort Bragg and environs

The entire town of Mendocino, a tiny woodframe village known for its Cape Cod architecture, is included on the National Register of Historic Places. (To get oriented, start at the Ford House interpretive centre on Main and take the walking tour, *see pp138–9.*) Once a lumber 'dog-hole port' and more recently an artists' enclave, modern-day Mendocino has become a north-coast tourist mecca with abundant small shops. More fascinating is exploring the area's small state parks, starting with **Mendocino Headlands**. For more information, contact **Mendocino Headland State Park**

(*PO Box 440, Mendocino, CA 95460; tel: (707) 937 5804; www.parks.ca.gov*).

Nearby is working-class **Fort Bragg**, a small city noted for its botanical gardens, the fine fresh seafood 'off the boat', its North Coast Brewing Company, and the Skunk Train ride to Willits (*see p143*).

For more information, contact the Fort Bragg-Mendocino Coast Chamber of Commerce (*217 S. Main St, PO Box 1141, Fort Bragg, CA 95437; tel: (707) 961 6300; www.mendocinocoast.com*).

South of Mendocino then inland via Highway 128 is the fascinating **Anderson Valley** area, a surviving farming area centred on Boonville. The area is noted for its almost-lost local

Gracious living at the McCallum House Bed & Breakfast, Mendocino

dialect of Boontling, its Buckhorn Saloon brewpub, and the **Mendocino County Fair and Apple Show** (one of the last non-commercial county fairs remaining in North America).

The Lost Coast

The wild coast north of Mendocino eventually becomes so rugged that the Coast Highway avoids it and veers inland to join Highway 101. For the truly adventurous, California's 'Lost Coast' is accessible via various narrow roads and routes starting from Garberville-Redway, Humboldt Redwoods and Ferndale. For information, stop by the visitor centre at **Humboldt Redwoods State Park** (*tel: (707) 946 2263; www.parks.ca.gov*) between Weott and Myers Flat – or write to them at the address given in the box below or contact **Sinkyone Wilderness State Park** (*1600 US 101 #8, Garberville, CA 95542; tel: (707) 986 7711; www.parks.ca.gov*).

The redwood parks

The north coast's finest feature, its virgin groves of *Sequoia sempervirens* or coastal redwoods, is best appreciated in Humboldt and Del Norte counties. Hugging Highway 101 just north of Garberville and Redway is **Humboldt Redwoods State Park**, with 20,234 hectares (50,000 acres) of almost unvisited redwood groves and upland grasslands brushed with mixed conifers and oaks. There are traditional tourist attractions too, especially along the old

highway's **Avenue of the Giants**. Most notable, in Myers Flat, is the **Shrine Drive-Thru Tree**, one of the state's oldest tourist attractions (wagon trains once drove through it).

Further north, beyond the fascinations of the small Victorian village of **Ferndale** and the attractions of adjacent **Eureka** and **Arcata**, are almost unseen treasures. **Redwood National Park**, which now incorporates three exceptional state parks, protects most of what remains of California's original 800,000 hectares (2 million acres) of virgin coastal redwoods (plus much over-logged acreage). Home to three of the world's six largest trees (including the tallest, 115m (379ft) 'Hyperion' Redwood), over 1,000 species of animal and plant life thrive here, including rare Roosevelt elk and (offshore, in season) California grey whales.

REDWOOD MISCELLANY

For more information, contact:
Humboldt Redwoods State Park
PO Box 100, Weott, CA 95571. Tel: (707) 946 2263; www.parks.ca.gov
Redwood National Park
Thomas H. Kuchel Visitor Center, US 101, Orick. Tel: (707) 465 7765. (For written information: 1111 Second St, Crescent City, CA 95531; tel: (707) 464 6101.)

Information about Prairie Creek, Del Norte Coast, and Jedediah Smith Redwoods State Parks, all included within the national park, is also provided by the Orick Center and at *www.parks.ca.gov*

Walk: Mendocino Headlands

This windswept town on the often fog-shrouded bluffs overlooking the Pacific could easily be mistaken for New England rather than California. In fact, film-makers have been using Mendocino as a New England lookalike since Johnny Belinda *was made there over 60 years ago.*

This walk explores not only the historic buildings but also the wild, rugged coast of the Mendocino Headlands.

Allow 1 hour plus sights.

Driving north on Highway 1, turn off at the first Mendocino exit on to Main St. The walk starts at the Presbyterian Church on the left-hand side of the road.

1 Mendocino Presbyterian Church

This is one of the oldest Presbyterian churches in continuous operation in California. In 1947 it was the set for *Johnny Belinda*, starring Jane Wyman.

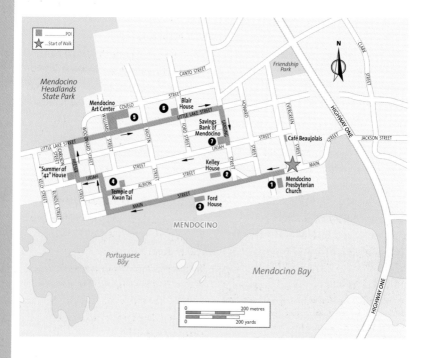

Continue along Main St, past Lansing St to Kelley House, set back from the street on the right-hand side.

2 Kelley House Museum

Built in 1861, Kelley House is now a Victorian museum and houses the Mendocino Historical Research Library.
Continue along Main Street – Ford House is on the left.

3 Ford House

Also a museum, Ford House was built in 1854 and houses the town's Visitor Information Bureau. There is an excellent large-scale model showing Mendocino as it was early last century. Many of the original wooden buildings of Mendocino have been destroyed by fire, and this is one of the oldest still standing.
Cross Main St again and walk past the boutiques and galleries to Woodward St. Turn right and right again on to Albion St.

Ford House and garden, Mendocino

4 The Temple of Kwan Tai

This small red building houses an old Chinese temple that can be visited by appointment only (*tel: (707) 937 5123; www.kwantaitemple.org*).
Return to Woodward St, turn right, walk to Ukiah St, turn left and continue to Heeser St. The old house on the corner of Heeser and Ukiah was the set for the film The Summer of '42. *Turn right on to Heeser and walk up to Little Lake St. Continue to Williams St.*

5 Mendocino Art Center

The Art Center has achieved a national reputation, and a small gallery has exhibitions of both local and national artists.
Continue along Little Lake St to Ford St.

6 Blair House

Mendocino is full of charming bed-and-breakfast inns. Blair House has the added attraction that it was the location for the television series *Murder, She Wrote*, starring Angela Lansbury.
Continue to Lansing St and turn right. Stay on the right-hand side of the street and walk to the corner of Ukiah St.

7 Savings Bank of Mendocino

This former Masonic Temple is topped by a superb redwood sculpture of *Father Time*.
Turn right on to Ukiah and walk to Heeser St. Turn left, go to Main St and take the trail to the headlands. Steps lead down from the bluff to Portuguese Beach.

Getting away from it all

California has an activity for practically anyone, from outdoor enthusiasts, who can choose from such activities as biking, kayaking, horse riding and caving, to those who enjoy sightseeing from a different perspective, such as hot-air balloon rides, wine touring on trains and island-hopping via ferries.

Angel Island

This is the largest island in San Francisco Bay and can easily be seen to the left of Alcatraz.

Angel Island is covered with forest, and herds of deer roam free. It was the Ellis Island of the west, used as a quarantine station for Asian immigrants. During World War II it was used as an internment camp for Japanese Americans, and the old buildings have been converted into a museum.

Visit the island for picnics, cycling and hiking. The hike around the island is 10km (6 miles) long and from the top there are 360-degree views of the Bay Area. It can be beautifully tranquil as no motor vehicles are allowed on the island. Access is by ferry from Pier 39 in San Francisco. It operates daily in the summer and at weekends during winter.

Contact: **Blue and Gold Fleet**, *Pier 39, San Francisco. Tel: (415) 705 8200. www.blueandgoldfleet.com*

Ballooning

Hot-air ballooning is a popular diversion in various California locales, perhaps most notably in Napa Valley to the north of San Francisco. One company, the oldest wine country ballooning firm, offers dawn launches followed by brunch with sparkling wines for refreshment.

Contact: **Napa Valley Balloons, Inc** *6795 Washington St, Yountville, CA 94599. Tel: (707) 944 0228 or toll-free (800) 253 2224. www.napavalley balloons.com*

Other highly regarded balloon outfits in Napa offering similar packages are the **Bonaventura Balloon Company** (*tel: (800) 359 6272; www.bonaventuraballoons.com*) and **Adventures Aloft** (*tel: (707) 944 4400; www.nvaloft.com*).

In southern California, the high desert around Temecula is quite popular for high-flying balloonists. **California Dreamin'** is a good choice (*tel: (800) 373 3359; www.californiadreamin.com*).

Bikes and Segways

In summer, alpine ski enthusiasts can schuss down the slopes on mountain bikes, a popular new pastime now that many resorts are exploring year-round recreation options. **Mammoth Mountain** on the Sierra Nevada's eastern slope offers 145km (90 miles) of ski runs 'groomed' in summer for cycle touring.

There are many bike trails in parks throughout California. If that sounds too strenuous, save your legs and take a Segway (electric vehicle) tour. In San Francisco, contact the **San Francisco and Sausalito Electric Tour Company** (*tel: (415) 474 3130; www.sfelectrictour. com*); in Sacramento try **Hysterical Walks and Rides** (*www.hysterical walks.com*).

Blue Goose Murder Mystery

The small steam-powered Blue Goose excursion train in the town of Yreka,

north of Mount Shasta, offers seasonal family fun and a very special summer adventure. An annual summer fund-raising benefit, the day-long Murder on the Blue Goose Express mystery tour, includes train fare, two meals, and even a party afterwards. Participants each receive a 'script' for their part in the drama and are expected to wear period attire. Reservations essential. Contact: **Yreka Western Railroad**, *300 E Miner St, Yreka, CA 96097. Tel: (800) 973 5277. www.yrekawesternrr.com*

Fabulous Filoli

Woodside is a rural oasis on the San Francisco peninsula. This exclusive community close to Stanford is home to one of the great 'stately' homes of California.

The 43-room mansion at Filoli was designed by Willis Polk in 1916 and, although the house is well worth a

Moody skies over the Lava Beds National Park

visit, it is the 6.5 hectares (16 acres) of themed, formal, enclosed gardens that are the main attraction. Eighteen gardeners were required for their maintenance, and none of their former glory has disappeared. Reservations are required for tours: *tel: (650) 364 8300; www.filoli.org*

Farm festivals

Unusual and sometimes highly entertaining in California is the multitude of community farm festivals that have sprouted up and gained tremendous popularity over the years. Most famous, perhaps, is the annual Gilroy Garlic Festival south of San Jose, where 150,000-plus people descend to celebrate the stinking rose with samples of garlic perfume and all-you-can-eat garlic ice cream (a few gallons are usually quite sufficient to feed the entire crowd) as well as big bands and other entertainment.

Other regional festivals include the Artichoke Festival in Castroville, the Great Monterey Squid Festival, the Stockton Asparagus Festival and the Monterey Bay Strawberry Festival. Even more obscure are events such as the California Prune Festival in Yuba City, the Pear Fair in Courtland and Isleton's Crawdad Festival. California also offers a wide array of colourful ethnic events.

A current events calendar, a listing of ethnic events and a listing of local chambers of commerce (best sources for obscure events information) can be obtained from **California Tourism** *PO Box 1499, Sacramento, CA 95812. Tel: (916) 444 4429. www.visitcalifornia.com*

Horsing around

What better way to appreciate the glory of the eastern Sierra and Yosemite than from the saddle of a horse? Various companies offer pack trips lasting anything from one hour to several days. Reputable firms include **Frontier Pack Train** (*tel: (888) 437 6853; www.frontierpacktrain.com*), **Virginia Lakes Pack Outfit** (*tel: (760) 937 0326; www.virginialakes.com*) and **Mammoth Lakes Pack Outfit** (*tel: (888) 475 8747; www.mammothpack.com*). They generally operate from late spring to early autumn. A full list of companies can be obtained from: **Eastern High Sierra Packers Association**, Bishop Chamber of Commerce, *690 N Main St, Bishop, CA 93514. Tel: (760) 873 8405. www.bishopvisitor.com*

Kayaking

Perhaps the most unobtrusive way of getting close to nature is silently gliding on water. It takes skill, but even novices can learn in a lesson or two to manage most day-long outings (depending on weather conditions). Contact: **Blue Waters Kayaking** *60 Fourth St, #C, Point Reyes Station, CA 94956. Tel: (415) 669 2600. www.bwkayak.com* **Kayak Tahoe** *PO Box 550399, S Lake*

Riding in Yosemite National Park

Portal, CA 95318. Tel: (209) 379 2317.
www.yosemiteconservancy.org

Riding a skunk in the daylight
The Skunk Train from Fort Bragg to Willits goes back to the area's lumbering heyday. The full 64km (40-mile) route offers cliff-hanging scenery and sky-high trestle travel through the Noyo River Gulch. The old steam Super Skunk engine chugs out only on Saturday half-day runs; a diesel engine pulls the load on longer and summer outings. On full-day trips, it is also possible to start and end in Willits. **Skunk Train** *Tel: (866) 457 5865. www.skunktrain.com*

Russian River road tour
Just over an hour's drive north from San Francisco is the Russian River resort area, offering an eclectic cultural mix. Very popular for tours is **Korbel Champagne Cellars** (*tel: (707) 824 7000; www.korbel.com*) on River Road, a few kilometres east of Guerneville. Noted for its champagnes, this vintage 1886 red-brick building (with lovely gardens) is the only outlet for the company's table wines. Just north of Guerneville are **Armstrong Redwoods State Natural Reserve** and the adjacent **Austin Creek State Recreation Area** (for both *tel: (707) 869 2015; www.parks.ca.gov*).

Some people prefer canoeing: **Burke's Canoe Trips** in Forestville offers quite reasonable day-long tours

Tahoe, CA 96155. Tel: (530) 544 2011.
www.kayaktahoe.com
Monterey Bay Kayaks *693 Del Monte Ave, Monterey, CA 93940. Tel: toll-free, 800 649 5357. www.montereybay kayaks.com*

Mono Lake and environmental education
The Mono Lake Committee – environmental activists who battle, in the courts and through the media, with Los Angeles Water and Power over the future of the lake's watershed – offers an array of seminars and classes.
Contact: **Mono Lake Committee** *PO Box 29, Lee Vining, CA 93541. Tel: (760) 647 6595. www.monolake.org*
Yosemite Conservancy *PO Box 230, El*

(*Cont. on p146*)

Ghost towns

The very mention of ghost towns can conjure up memories of old Westerns, bleached bones lying in the desert and tumbleweed blowing through deserted ruins.

California has its fair share of these abandoned settlements. Whenever a mine ran out of gold or silver the town that grew up around it would lose its population. The mines were never in the most hospitable parts of the state and there was absolutely no reason for anyone to live in these God-forsaken places unless there was money to be made.

The buildings usually fell into decay within a few years, and often all that can be found now are rusty tin cans, barbed wire and the overgrown foundations of a few houses, though occasionally some buildings survive. The most popular and accessible ghost town lies just outside Barstow on the road between Los Angeles and Las Vegas.

In 1881 Calico boomed with 20 saloons and its own Chinatown. Over $86 million of gold and silver was mined before the mines were exhausted.

Walter Knott of Knott's Berry Farm restored the town and handed it over to San Bernardino County who now operate it as a kind of ghost town theme park. In spite of its blatantly commercial atmosphere, you can still

Abandoned buildings at Bodie Ghost Town, Bodie State Historic Park

Church at Calico Ghost Town, Yermo

get a feel for the harsh life of the miners in these barren mountains.

In 1904, on the edge of Death Valley, a gold strike near Rhyolite resulted in the population growing to 10,000 in a few months. By 1911 the city was reduced to a handful.

Just outside the northwest boundary of Death Valley, Rhyolite today is a group of ruined façades. The front of the Cook Bank Building provides the perfect symbol of a ghost town for photographers, and a few other ruins line the once busy main street. In 1906 Tom Kelly built a house out of 51,000 bottles. Not only is this still standing but it is still inhabited. Inside is an odd collection of antiques and relics.

Bodie is one of the jewels of California. High in the Eastern Sierra at the end of a long stretch of dirt road off Highway 395, Bodie stands as a remarkably well-preserved example of a classic ghost town. Until 1876 it was a thriving mining community. Today 170 houses still stand and you can wander through streets that have remained unchanged for decades.

This outdoor museum has been designated a State Historic Park, and, although there has been little renovation, the buildings have been preserved from further deterioration. Many of the buildings are open and many are still complete with furniture and personal belongings. There is a feeling of total authenticity here, particularly when trying to breathe the thin mountain air at 2,590m (8,500ft) as you climb the steep streets. Opposite the town is a cemetery that graphically documents the lives of the miners.

(*tel: (707) 887 1222; www.burkescanoe trips.com*). Others prefer following the river inland to visit abundant and excellent area wineries. Still others consider the Russian River an annual event and visit only in September, during the popular Jazz and Blues festival (*www.omegaevents.com*).
Contact: **Russian River Chamber of Commerce** (*PO Box 331, Guerneville, CA 95441; tel: (707) 869 9000; www.russianriver.com*). The walk-in visitor centre is at *16209 First Street, Guerneville*. For a free map and brochure about area wineries contact the **Russian River Wine Road** (*PO Box 46, Healdsburg, CA 95448; tel: (800) 723 6336. www.wineroad.com*).

Sailing on horseback

The one-time ranch of noted American adventurer and author Jack London is preserved as an exceptional historic park. With his wife Charmian, London regularly travelled the grasslands and wooded canyons of his beloved Beauty Ranch on horseback. 'I am a sailor on horseback!' he once declared. Especially enjoyable today, and historically appropriate, are the horse-riding trips offered here.
Contact: **Triple Creek Horse Outfit** (*tel: (707) 887 8700; www.triplecreek horseoutfit.com*).

In the Russian River's Armstrong Redwoods another company offers half-day to three-day horse-riding trips, as noted for the campfire cuisine as for the well-mannered mountain-savvy

Visit Napa Valley on the Wine Train

horses. Contact: **Armstrong Woods Pack Station** (*PO Box 287, Guerneville, CA 95446, tel: (707) 887 2939*).

In Big Sur, rides in Andrew Molera State Park and longer into the Ventana Wilderness are offered by **Molera Horseback Tours** who have certified guides to navigate this 1,942-hectare (4,800-acre) coastal paradise.
Molera Horseback Tours, *Andrew Molera State Park, Big Sur, CA 93920. Tel: (831) 625 5486. www.molera horsebacktours.com*

Spelunking into Middle Earth

California has fascinating caves and caverns to explore, most of them in the Gold Country foothills. All offer a civilised descent via steps or stairways. A few also allow adventurers to abseil down into the primal darkness.

East of San Andreas, visitors to **California Cavern** (*tel: (866) 762 2837; www.caverntours.com*) can spurn the commercial 'trail of lights' at this state historic landmark and instead squeeze through muddy fissures to reach hidden caves and underground lakes (hardhats, overalls, rafts and guides provided). To the south, near Murphys, **Mercer Caverns** (*tel: (209) 728 2101; www.mercercaverns.com*) is strictly a family destination. But at **Moaning Cavern** near Angels Camp (*tel: (866) 762 2837; www.caverntours.com*) no experience is required for the more exciting abseil route or full caving tour. (This cave is reputedly the largest in California.) Hundreds of kilometres north are the **Lake Shasta Caverns** (*tel: (800) 795 2283; www.lakeshasta caverns.com*). Abseiling or rappelling tours of these colourful caves are by advance booking only.

Santa Catalina Island

A mere 35km (22 miles) off the coast near Long Beach, Santa Catalina Island provides within its 90km (56 miles) of coastline a pristine wilderness that rises to over 610m (2,000ft) in elevation in the interior.

Visitors take the ferry from Long Beach to Avalon, the only town on the island. Maps and information can be obtained from the **Santa Catalina Island Chamber of Commerce and Visitors' Bureau**, on the Green Pleasure Pier (*tel: (310) 510 1520; www.catalina chamber.com*). Glass-bottom-boat tours are available from several kiosks along Green Pleasure Pier. The **Santa Catalina Island Company** (*tel: (310) 510 8687; www.visitcatalinaisland.com*) has night tours, when floodlights are

used to attract the marine life. The **Catalina Safari Bus** service (*tel: (310) 510 2800; www.visitcatalinaisland.com*) drops off hikers at various points around the island. Bicycles can be rented from **Brown's Bikes** at *107 Pebbly Beach Rd, Avalon* (*tel: (310) 510 0986; www.catalinabiking.com*).

The Wine Train

A popular activity with tourists is the Wine Train. All runs head north from the city of Napa to St Helena, where passengers disembark for winery tours by bus. More expensive trips include food served in the dining cars, while hors d'oeuvres and wine tasting are offered in the lounge cars. Contact: **Napa Valley Wine Train** (*1275 McKinstry St, Napa, CA 94559; tel: (800) 427 4124; www.winetrain.com*).

Whale-watching

From mid-December until the end of February, California grey whales make their annual 9,656km (6,000-mile) migration from Alaska to Mexico. They return between March and mid-May.

These huge mammals can be seen from many of the promontories along the coast, or, for a more intimate experience, travel out to meet them in a small boat. Whale-watching cruises are run by several companies, including **The Oceanic Society** (*toll-free tel: (800) 326 7491; www.oceanicsociety.org*) and **Sea Landing** (*tel: (888) 779 4253; www.condorcruises.com*), whose Condor Cruises are very popular.

Shopping

Like most of America, California is a shopper's dream. Not only can you find anything and everything, from popular brand names to unusual imported items, but the price will be attractive too.

WHAT TO BUY
Clothes

Both men's and women's clothes are available in a wide variety of styles and prices, from French designer dresses and Savile Row suits to denim jeans. There are some incredible bargains to be found if you know where to look.

JC Penney and **Target** are both department store chains with inexpensive clothes. Nothing here approaches *haute couture* but for work clothes they are difficult to beat.

At the other end of the department store ladder are **Macy's**, **Neiman Marcus**, **Nordstrom** and **Saks Fifth Avenue**, which have designer clothes and recognised brand names. These stores often have good sales.

There are several discount clothing stores that offer the best bargains of all. They all sell name brands, very often designer labels, and often factory seconds. They may not have a wide range of sizes available in all styles but their prices more than make up for the lack of choice.

US-founded chains selling trendy fashion include **Abercrombie & Fitch**, **American Apparel**, **Banana Republic** and **Gap**. For cheap, Top Shop-style clothes, head to **Forever 21** or H&M; for stylish mid-range womenswear, go to **J Crew**.

For the latest fashion from the couture houses, there's no shortage of shops (Beverly Hills' Rodeo Drive being the most famous location), but expect heavy dents in your credit card.

Electronic goods

Remember that all equipment powered by mains electricity will be for 110v at 60 cycles, but battery-powered gadgets use internationally available battery sizes.

As the home of America's hi-tech industry, California has plenty of computers, accessories and software at bargain prices. Determine compatibility with overseas systems first. **Best Buy** and **Circuit City** specialise in electronics; the self-explanatory **Apple** store is another draw.

Photographic equipment

The US is one of the cheapest places in the world to buy cameras and lenses, but always check online for the lowest prices first. The Internet is an invaluable source of information.

Cameras in the US frequently have a different designation from the rest of the world, so check on the specifications before you leave home.

Books, music and DVDs

Discounting books has become an accepted practice in the US and many newly published works are available at substantial discounts.

Borders and **Barnes & Noble** are both reputable chains found across California. Most major shops sell CDs and DVDs, but note that most commercial DVDs won't work back home unless you have a multi-region DVD player. In terms of independent record stores, the mighty **Amoeba Music** on Haight Street in San Francisco can sustain hours of browsing.

Souvenirs

Apart from the obvious printed T-shirt and mugs, there is little that is unique to California. Gold nugget jewellery is a popular souvenir of the Gold Country, and 'grow your own redwood' kits make interesting mementoes – if you have room for the world's tallest tree!

For the sports fan, clothing in the colours of both major baseball and American football clubs is available at most sports outfitters.

Outlet malls

These huge malls, containing discount designer stores, are destinations in their own right. Among the best are **Desert Hills Premium Outlets** near Palm Springs. *48400 Seminole Dr, Cabazon. Tel: (951) 849 6641. www.premium outlets.com. Open: Sun–Thur 10am– 8pm, Fri 10am–9pm, Sat 9am–9pm.*

WHERE TO SHOP
Greater Los Angeles

Southern California is the home of vast shopping malls. Recommended ones include **Del Amo Fashion Center** (*3525 Carson St, Torrance; tel: (310) 542 8525; www.simon.com; open: daily 10am–7pm*), **Glendale Galleria** (*100 W. Broadway, Suite 700, Glendale; tel: (818) 246 6737; www.glendalegalleria.com; open: Mon–Sat 10am–9pm, Sun 11am–7pm*) and, in particular, **South Coast Plaza** (*3333 Bristol St, Costa Mesa; tel: (800) 782 8888; www.southcoastplaza.com; open: Mon–Fri 10am–9pm, Sat 10am–8pm, Sun 11am–6.30pm*), which includes a Bloomingdale's department store.

Beverly Center

This is a 3-hectare (8-acre) shopping mall filled with upmarket shops, department stores and restaurants. *8500 Beverly Blvd, Los Angeles. Tel: (310) 854 0070. www.beverlycenter.com. Open: Mon–Sat 10am–9pm, Sun 11am–8pm.*

The Grove

Next to the Farmers Market, this lovely open-air mall is home to shops and restaurants, as well as a decent cinema.

189 The Grove Dr, Los Angeles. Tel: (323) 900 8080. www.thegrovela. com. Open: Mon–Thur 10am–9pm, Fri & Sat 10am–10pm, Sun 10am–8pm.

Rodeo Drive
The name is synonymous with wealth. Window-shopping along this super-exclusive street is enough for most people. Some shops admit customers by appointment only.

San Diego
Bazaar del Mundo
This Mexican market within Old Town San Diego State Historic Park has a wide range of colourful crafts.

4002 Wallace St, San Diego. Tel: (619) 220 5422. www.parks.ca.gov. Open: daily 10am–7pm.

Seaport Village
Around 50 shops occupy this waterfront development with great views across the bay, close to downtown San Diego.

849 W. Harbor Dr, San Diego. Tel: (619) 235 4014. www.seaportvillage.com. Open: daily 10am–9pm.

Westfield Horton Plaza
This user-friendly outdoor mall has over 130 shops and restaurants.

324 Horton Plaza, San Diego. Tel: (619) 239 8180. www.westfield.com. Open: Mon–Fri 10am–9pm, Sat 10am–8pm, Sun 11am–7pm.

San Francisco
The Cannery
This converted canning factory has three floors of shops and restaurants.

2801 Leavenworth St, San Francisco. Tel: (415) 771 3112. www.thecannery.com

Crocker Galleria
The Galleria in Milan was the model for this glass-domed collection of fashionable shops.

1 Montgomery St, San Francisco.

The Chinatown gate at the corner of Grant Avenue, San Francisco

Tel: (415) 393 1505. www.thecrocker galleria.com. Open: Mon–Fri 10am–6pm, Sat 10am–5pm.

Ghirardelli Square

Ghirardelli still has its chocolate shop here, but most of the square has been transformed into an interesting mixture of boutiques, galleries and restaurants.
900 N Point St, San Francisco. Tel: (415) 775 5500. www.ghirardellisq.com. Open: Mon–Thur 10am–6pm, Fri & Sat 10am–9pm, Sun 11am–6pm.

Maiden Lane

Exclusive boutiques and galleries line this charming lane off Union Square. No 140 was designed by Frank Lloyd Wright.

Pier 39

Street performers entertain the shoppers on this old San Francisco cargo wharf that has plenty of shops, restaurants and resident-but-wild sea lions.
Beach St & The Embarcadero, San Francisco. Tel: (415) 705-5500. www.pier39.com. Open: daily 10am–8pm.

Sutter Street

For four blocks, from the 300s to the 700s, Sutter Street has some of the most exclusive fashion boutiques and galleries.

Union Square

If San Francisco has a centre, then this is it. All the major department stores are here, including **Saks Fifth Avenue**, **Macy's** and **Neiman Marcus**.

Union Street

This street in Cow Hollow is full of fashionable boutiques and restaurants.

Other areas
Bakersfield

The downtown antiques district on 19th Street has interesting shops to browse through for treasures and trinkets.

Fresno

This valley town is known for its street-side fruit stalls, though the **River Park** shopping centre has a good selection of stores and a popular movie theatre.
40 El Camino, Fresno. Tel: (559) 437 4855. www.shopriverpark.com. Open: daily, varied hours depending on retailer.

Sacramento

Arden Fair Mall has over 165 shops and is probably your best bet in this state capital.
1689 Arden Way, Sacramento. Tel: (916) 920 1199. www.ardenfair.com. Open: Mon–Sat 10am–9pm, Sun 11am–7pm.

San Luis Obispo

Avila Valley Barn is a good place to pick up fresh fruit, home-made baked goods and ice cream, and they have a seasonal pick-your-own garden as well.
560 Avila Beach Dr, San Luis Obispo. Tel: (805) 595 2816. www.avilavalley barn.com. Open: daily 9am–6pm from May to Dec.

Entertainment

In the state that is the centre of the world's film industry, there is no shortage of talent waiting to make its mark on the world of entertainment. It seems that every restaurant in Los Angeles is staffed by actors and actresses just waiting to be discovered.

Both London West End and Broadway shows are regularly featured at theatres in Los Angeles and San Francisco, and these are complemented by a multitude of small theatres producing both experimental and traditional drama. Comedy clubs are particularly good.

Classical fans are well catered for with world-class opera, ballet and symphony orchestras. The Performing Arts Center of Los Angeles County contains the architecturally jaw-dropping Frank Gehry-designed **Walt Disney Concert Hall**, home of the LA Philharmonic. The centre also houses the **Dorothy Chandler Pavilion** (base of the LA Opera), the **Ahmanson** (*see right*) and the smaller **Mark Taper Forum**.

Entertainment pages of newspapers usually list and review current events.

Day-of-performance tickets are available at half price from the **TIX Bay Area booth** in Union Square (*tel: (415) 433 7827*).

MAJOR THEATRES
Los Angeles
Ahmanson Theatre
135 N Grand Ave. Tel: (213) 972 7211. www.musiccenter.org
Geffen Playhouse
10886 Le Conte Ave. Tel: (310) 208 5454. www.geffenplayhouse.com

San Diego
La Jolla Playhouse
UCSD Campus. Tel: (858) 550 1010. www.lajollaplayhouse.org
Old Globe Theater
Balboa Park. Tel: (619) 234 5623. www.oldglobe.org

San Francisco
American Conservatory Theatre
405 Geary St. Tel: (415) 749 2228. www.act-sf.org
Curran Theatre
445 Geary St. Tel: (415) 551 2000.
Magic Theatre
Fort Mason Center, Marina Blvd. Tel: (415) 441 8822. www.magictheatre.org

COMEDY CLUBS
Los Angeles
The Comedy Store
8433 W Sunset Blvd. Tel: (323) 650 6268. www.thecomedystore.com
The Improv
8162 Melrose Ave. Tel: (323) 651 2583.

San Francisco
Cobb's
915 Columbus Ave. Tel: (415) 928 4320. www.cobbscomedy.com
The Punch Line
444 Battery St. Tel: (415) 397 4337. (Also in Sacramento.)

CLASSICAL MUSIC, BALLET AND OPERA
Los Angeles
Los Angeles Opera & Philharmonic
135 N Grand Ave. Tel: (213) 972 8001 & (323) 850 2000. www.musiccenter.org

San Diego
San Diego Opera
1200 3rd Ave. Tel: (619) 533 7000. www.sdopera.com
San Diego Symphony
1245 7th Ave. Tel: (619) 235 0804. www.sandiegosymphony.org

San Francisco
San Francisco Opera
301 Van Ness Ave. Tel: (415) 864 3330. www.sfopera.com
San Francisco Symphony
201 Van Ness Ave. Tel: (415) 864 6000. www.sfsymphony.org

JAZZ, BLUES AND ROCK
Los Angeles
Babe's & Ricky's Inn
4339 Leimert Blvd. Tel: (323) 295 9112.
The Viper Room
8852 W Sunset Blvd. Tel: (310) 358 1881. www.viperroom.com

San Diego
Belly Up
143 S Cedros Ave, Solana Beach. Tel: (858) 481 8140. www.bellyup.com

San Francisco
Great American Music Hall
859 O'Farrell St. Tel: (415) 885 0750. www.gamh.com
Jazz at Pearl's
256 Columbus Avenue. Tel: (415) 291 8255.

NIGHTCLUBS
Los Angeles
Avalon
1735 Vine St. Tel: (323) 462 8900. www.avalonhollywood.com

San Francisco
Bimbo's 365 Club
1025 Columbus Ave. Tel: (415) 474 0365. www.bimbos365club.com
DNA Lounge
375 11th St. Tel: (415) 626 1409. www.dnalounge.com
Mezzanine
444 Jessie St. Tel: (415) 625 8880. www.mezzaninesf.com
Slim's
333 11th St. Tel: (415) 255 0333. www.slims-sf.com

Children

California is a children's paradise. From Disneyland® to the Monterey Bay Aquarium, SeaWorld and San Diego Zoo, there is a multitude of activities to keep even the most jaded children amused for weeks. It would be impossible to cover everything here as almost every entry in the book would be suitable. Below are listed just a few of the attractions not mentioned elsewhere.

Note that, aside from Disneyland® and Knott's Berry Farm, many California theme parks are only open during the weekends in winter (daily in summer).

Alpine Meadows Stables
Scenic horse riding tours through Tahoe National Forest, for ages 5 and up.
355 Alpine Meadows Rd, Tahoe City. Tel: (530) 583 3905. www.alpinemeadowsstables.com. Open: daily May–Oct.

Aquarium of the Pacific
Explore the three regions of the Pacific Ocean with a collection of over 11,000 animals, including an interactive Shark Lagoon. A pleasant outdoor garden is on site also, featuring Californian native plants.
100 Aquarium Way, Long Beach. Tel: (562) 590 3100. www.aquariumofpacific.org. Open: daily 9am–6pm. Admission charge.

California's Great America
This park in Santa Clara County south of San Francisco offers over 55 attractions including 3 water rides.
4701 Great America Parkway, Santa Clara. Tel: (408) 988 1776. www.cagreatamerica.com. Open: daily Mar–Oct. Call for opening times. Admission charge.

Fairytale Town
A fun children's play park with a petting zoo and various interactive activities.
3901 Land Park Dr, Sacramento. Tel: (916) 808 7462. www.fairytaletown.org. Open: daily 9am–4pm Mar–Oct, Thur–Sun 10am–4pm Nov–Feb. Admission charge.

Safari West
This private wildlife preserve is home to warthogs, cheetahs and many other African species that can be viewed via 3-hour safari tours.
3115 Porter Creek Rd, Santa Rosa.

Tel: (707) 579 2551.
www.safariwest.com. Open: daily, with
scheduled tours starting at 9am.
Admission charge.

Sequoia Park Zoo

Good value and interesting for young
children, the zoo features a walk-
through aviary, petting zoo, rare red
pandas and an interactive forest exhibit.
3414 W St, Eureka.
Tel: (707) 441 4263.
www.sequoiaparkzoo.net.
Open: daily 10am–5pm, closed Mon in
winter. Admission charge.

Six Flags Discovery Kingdom

Not as celebrated as its Southern
California cousin, this park is
nonetheless worth a trip if you have
bored kids in tow. Children will enjoy
seeing the animals, while rides with
names such as V2: Vertical Velocity will
keep adrenalin junkies entertained.
1001 Fairgrounds Dr, Vallejo.
Tel: (707) 643 6722. www.sixflags.com.
Call for opening times. Admission charge.

Six Flags Magic Mountain and
Hurricane Harbor

Magic Mountain has over 100 rides,
games and attractions spread across 105
hectares (260 acres) and includes the
Colossus, once one of the biggest and
fastest wooden roller coasters in the
world. Hurricane Harbor, meanwhile,
has watery thrills aplenty.
26101 Magic Mountain Parkway,
Valencia. Tel: (661) 255 4100.

www.sixflags.com. Call for opening times.
Admission charge.

Turtle Bay Exploration Park

An entertaining educational centre with
a botanical garden, natural history and
science museum and a fair amount
animal exhibits.
840 Sundial Bridge Dr, Redding.
Tel: (800) 887 8532. www.turtlebay.org.
Call for opening times. Admission charge.

UC Botanical Garden at Berkeley

Expansive research gardens, fun for all
ages, with various tours focused on
older children, including a Foods of the
Americas tour in October where
food crops are displayed, discussed
and consumed.
200 Centennial Dr, Berkeley.
Tel: (510) 643 2755.
www.botanicalgarden.berkeley.edu.
Call for opening times. Admission charge.

Winchester Mystery House

Children love the bizarre and spooky
atmosphere of the house. It was built
by Sarah Winchester, heiress to the
Winchester rifle fortune, who believed
that she would live as long as the house
continued to grow. By the time she
died in 1922 the house had grown
to 160 rooms over 2.5 hectares
(6 acres).
525 S Winchester Blvd, San Jose.
Tel: (408) 247 2101.
www.winchestermysteryhouse.com.
Open: hours vary with the season.
Admission charge.

Sport and leisure

California is the home of champions, a breeding ground for athletes of every kind and a state with an unparalleled sports infrastructure. With its nearly ideal weather conditions and its penchant for the pursuit of perfection when it comes to all things physical, California is an athlete's mecca. It has over 20 major professional sports teams, dozens of minor-league teams, some of the best collegiate athletics in the country and a huge variety of opportunity for participant sports.

Nearly one-third of American athletes at the 2000 Summer Olympics were native Californians. They won 30 medals – 32 per cent of the US total. Author Herbert Gold observes 'This Dorado of escapees from elsewhere has produced a new race – the Californian. So much athletic grace is almost unnatural.' To be a good sport in California, you can either do it or just watch it. Whatever you choose, it is all around you.

Note that Ticketmaster and Tickets.com sell tickets to many games through their websites and through their outlets.

Spectator sports
American football
No other state can boast having as many professional football teams as California. They are the Oakland Raiders, the San Diego Chargers and the San Francisco 49ers. Four teams from the National Football League take to the field (called the gridiron) every

autumn from early September through to late December. Two lucky teams go all the way to the Super Bowl in late January/early February.

Recently, following decades of wins, the **San Francisco 49ers** have had weak seasons, though there are signs that their fortunes are turning around. Getting a ticket to a 49ers game is difficult, although you can occasionally get single-seat tickets.

The **Oakland Raiders**, too, have had less-than-stellar results in recent seasons, and tickets for their games are rarely sold out. They are notorious for their aggressive and hard-hitting style of football. They play at McAfee Coliseum, just off the I-880 at Oakland (*tel: (800) 724 3377*).

The **San Diego Chargers** battle on the field at Qualcomm Stadium (*tel: (619) 220 8497*).

College football is also quite enjoyable and accessible. In northern California, both Stanford University and the University of California at

Berkeley have strong football traditions. In southern California, the University of Southern California (USC), University of California at Los Angeles (UCLA) and San Diego State University (SDSU) are among a host of college teams to take the field. The USC Trojans, in particular, are highly rated.

Baseball

The American equivalent of cricket takes place at five major baseball league stadiums across California. The teams are the Los Angeles Angels of Anaheim, the Los Angeles Dodgers, the Oakland Athletics, the San Diego Padres and the San Francisco Giants.

The San Francisco Bay area is home to two of the nation's best teams, the **San Francisco Giants** and the **Oakland Athletics** (**A's**). The Giants swing their bats at AT & T Park (*tel: (877) 473 4849*). The Athletics play at the Oakland-Alameda County Coliseum (*tel: (877) 493 2255*), although they plan to move to a new state-of-the-art Cisco Field in San Jose during 2011.

In southern California the **Los Angeles Dodgers** enjoy an outstanding reputation in baseball although they have had erratic seasons recently. They play at Dodger Stadium in Echo Park (*tel: (866) 363 4377*).

The **Anaheim Angels** (officially the Los Angeles Angels of Anaheim) play at the Anaheim Stadium (*tel: (714) 663 9000*) and the **San Diego Padres** play at Petco Park (*tel: (619) 795 5000*).

Basketball

The regular National Basketball Association (NBA) season runs from late October/early November until April, with championship playoffs continuing until June. California's teams include the Golden State Warriors, the Los Angeles Clippers, the Los Angeles Lakers and the Sacramento Kings.

The **Golden State Warriors** play at the Oracle Archa in Oakland (*tel: (888) 479 4667*), while the **Sacramento Kings** play at the Arco Arena.

The Oakland A's in their current home, the Oakland-Alameda County Coliseum

The Galaxy score at the Home Depot Center

The **Los Angeles Clippers** have shown flashes of promise in recent years. They play at Staples Center (*tel: (619) 220 8497*).

The reigning champions of California basketball remain the **Los Angeles Lakers**, who also play at Staples Center in downtown LA. One of the greatest teams in the history of American sport, the Lakers have developed a following that literally spans the globe.

Football
Traditionally, football – called soccer here – hasn't had a big following in America, but interest was renewed in 2007 when a certain David Beckham made his debut for the **LA Galaxy** team, based at The Home Depot Center in Carson, just outside LA (*tel: (877) 342 5299; www.homedepotcenter.com*).

Motor racing
The famous **Mazda Raceway Laguna Seca** near Monterey features on the car and MotoGP racing calendar, as well as hosting other events.

Participatory sports
Golf
If you decide to bring your clubs on holiday, you will not be disappointed. Golf is a year-round sport in nearly all parts of California, and almost every city and town has a public golf course.

Notable public courses include: **Silverado Resort** in Napa, **Tilden Park** in Berkeley, **Rancho Park Golf Course** in Los Angeles, **Torrey Pines Golf Course** in La Jolla and the **Indian Canyons Golf Resort** in Palm Springs. Palm Springs is also home to the excellent **PGA West Golf Club & Resort**.

Skiing
Whether you are a downhill skier or a cross-country skier, California has some of the finest conditions in the US. From November to May, skiing in the Sierra Nevada has gathered a national following. It is almost always better than the cold, icy and crowded ski slopes of the East Coast; it is often every bit as good as the famed Rocky Mountain skiing.

The Lake Tahoe region boasts the highest concentration of skiing in the US. Resorts include **Squaw Valley USA**, **Heavenly Mountain**, **Kirkwood Mountain** and **Alpine Meadows**.

Further south is **Mammoth Mountain**, on the eastern side of the Sierras. It is one of the continent's largest ski areas, with 27 lifts and more than 150 trails, and with a vertical drop of 945m (3,100ft). Nearer Los Angeles, an assortment of ski areas includes **Mount Baldy**, **Big Bear**, **Snow Summit**, **Mount Waterman** and **Kratka Ridge**.

Cross-country skiing is also very popular in the Sierras. At Soda Springs, west of Lake Tahoe, is **Royal Gorge**, North America's largest Nordic ski centre. You can ski at a touring centre such as the **Kirkwood Cross Country and Snowshoe Center**, southwest of Lake Tahoe. For the more intrepid, a trip into the back country in one of the state's many mountain parks and reserves is a possibility.

Tennis

California is tennis crazy. At nearly every school and every park in California, players both old and young practise their skills in what might be the nation's leading tennis state.

From Pancho Gonzales and Jack Kramer to Billie Jean King and the Williams sisters, California has dominated the sport of tennis, at both professional and amateur levels.

More information on tennis can be obtained from the **Northern California Tennis Association** (*tel: (510) 748 7373*) or the **Southern California Tennis Association** (*tel: (310) 208 3838*).

Other sports

Watersports are very popular during the summer, including kayaking and white-water rafting. Surfing, together with windsurfing, still enjoy tremendous popularity, and scuba-diving trips are available at many places along the coast.

Cycling, both mountain biking and beach cruising, is a popular activity in California for locals and tourists alike.

Horses can be rented at stables located throughout the state, particularly on the coast where they can be ridden along the beach.

Fishing, last but certainly not least, is the state's most popular pastime, and almost every stretch of water, both fresh and sea, will have an angling club close by. Rods and other equipment are usually available for hire by the day at very reasonable rates.

Wherever there is a harbour along the coast someone will be offering fishing charters. Salmon is the most popular catch, followed by rock cod and bass.

Freshwater anglers have the choice of steelhead, salmon, sturgeon and trout. Most of the mountain areas have fitters offering fishing trips.

For current information on fishing licences and seasons, contact the California **Department of Fish and Game** (*1416 Ninth St, Sacramento, CA 95814; tel: (916) 445 0411; www.dfg.ca.gov*).

See also Getting away on pp140–47.

Food and drink

There is virtually no cuisine on earth that cannot be found in California. San Francisco alone has over 4,000 restaurants, even more per capita than New York. Californians enjoy eating, not just for the sake of it but for the love of it. It is a state of 'foodies' who have helped California become one of the world's great gastronomic centres. Fine restaurants abound, and not just in the cities.

CALIFORNIA CUISINE
Breakfast

From diners to top restaurants and hotel lounges, the breakfast menu in California is vast. Choices can include omelettes with hash browns and toast, pancakes or waffles topped with fruit and whipped cream, and eggs served with bacon, sausage or ham. Lighter choices include yoghurt and muesli, acai bowls (a healthy Brazilian berry topped with granola, fruit and honey), a bagel, pastry or fruit smoothie.

Dinner

This is the main meal of the day for most Californians, and for most Americans for that matter. Dinner is served from 5.30pm to 10.30pm and the choice of dishes is vast.

Sweets and snacks

Cupcakes, fresh pies and rich pastries are found in many good bakeries. Those with a sweet tooth should seek out **Krispy Kreme** doughnuts and **Sprinkles** cupcake shops – found mainly around LA – and **See's Candies**, which are sold throughout the state and make great souvenirs.

Diners

The diner is an American institution. They are similar to coffee shops, serving a generic menu of fast food, including burgers, sandwiches, omelettes and salads. The traditional diner was designed to look like a railroad dining car with lots of chrome and a jukebox. Ubiquitous chains include **Denny's** and **Mel's Drive-In**. Despite the name, these restaurants are no longer drive-in, but they do provide a welcome slice of Americana.

Fast food

Fast-food chains abound and many of them are so international that they have become synonymous with American food.

There are several big-name look-alikes, including **Wendy's**, **Carl's Jr** and

Jack in the Box (all **£**). They all provide variations of the same products at more or less the same (low) price.

DRINKS
Wine
The wine industry extends from the great vineyards of Napa and Sonoma up to Lake and Mendocino counties in the north and as far south as San Diego. Excellent wines are made near Santa Cruz and Santa Barbara that are the equal of many European fine wines. Many of the grapevines in fact descend from European stock.

Beer
America's contribution to the wine industry unfortunately did not spill over to beer. To Europeans, American beer is fizzy and tasteless. Fortunately, northern California produces several of the best beers in the US from small local breweries. Sierra Nevada Pale Ale from Chico and San Francisco's Anchor Steam Beer are both excellent.

Other drinks
In non-alcoholic drinks colas lead the market and all the usual suspects are readily available. Root beer also has a loyal following and connoisseurs rank A&W as one of the best.

Bars
The American bar is certainly a place for serious drinking. The more atmospheric ones are dark and dramatic – some of the best are found in posh hotels, such as the Redwood Room at the Clift in San Francisco, while the Old Hollywood-style Musso & Frank Grill in Los Angeles is legendary.

When buying alcohol, whether in a supermarket, drugstore, liquor store, pub or bar, don't be surprised if you are asked for photo ID even if you are over 21 (the legal drinking age in California). Some places have a policy of asking anyone who looks under the age of 40!

WHERE TO EAT
The restaurant business has always been precarious and has become increasingly so in the present economic climate. New restaurants open and close with monotonous regularity, so ask locally for recommendations.

Compared with Europe, even the most expensive restaurants will seem reasonably priced. One thing to bear in mind, however, is that portions here are massive. You can easily share a main dish (entrée) between two, although, annoyingly, some restaurants levy a 'split charge'.

The potent Mexican spirit is made from the distilled fermented juice of an agave plant

The following key is an indication of restaurant price. The price rating indicates the approximate cost per person for a three-course meal without alcohol.

£   under $15
££ $15–25
£££ $25–50
££££ over $50

SOUTHERN CALIFORNIA

Los Angeles

Concert Hall Café ££
Located inside LA's Walt Disney Concert Hall, this Patina group restaurant offers gourmet salads, sandwiches, desserts and drinks.
111 S Grand Ave, Los Angeles. Tel: (213) 972 3550. www.patinagroup. com. Open: daily 11.30am–2.30pm (on performance days 5pm–intermission).

Father's Office ££
Some of the best burgers and sweet potato fries (chips) in the state, with a cosy décor.
1018 Montana Ave, Santa Monica. Tel: (310) 736 2224. www.fathersoffice.com. Open: Mon–Thur 5pm–1am, Fri 4pm–2am, Sat noon–2am, Sun noon–midnight.

The Urth Caffe ££
Great coffees, teas and organic pies. Serious celebrity-sighting spot.
8565 Melrose Ave, West Hollywood. Tel: (310) 659 0628. www.urthcaffe.com. Open: Mon–Thur & Sun 6.30am–11.30pm, Fri & Sat 6.30am–midnight.

Musso & Frank Grill £££
Old-school Hollywood glamour with loyal waiters and an atmospheric, vintage interior dating back to 1919. Try the Welsh rarebit, chicken pot pie and other classics.
6667 Hollywood Blvd, Los Angeles. Tel: (323) 467 7788. Open: Tue–Thur 11am–11pm, Fri & Sat 11am–late.

The Ivy ££££
The quintessential LA celebrity hangout. The food is secondary to the locale but it's still good (save room for dessert).
113 N Robertson Blvd, Los Angeles. Tel: (310) 274 8303. Open: Mon–Sat 11.30am–10.30pm, Sun 10.30am–10.30pm.

Napa Rose ££££
Another great restaurant in an unlikely place – Disneyland® Resort. Excellent wine list.
1600 S Disneyland Dr, Anaheim. Tel: (714) 781 3463. www.disneyland.com. Open: daily 5.30–10pm.

San Diego

Hodad's £
Huge delicious burgers and tiny prices in a funky surfer shack that's been around for decades.
5010 Newport Ave, Ocean Beach. Tel: (619) 224 4623. www.hodadies.com. Open: Sun–Thur 11am–9pm, Fri & Sat 11am–10pm.

The Mission ££
Great for breakfast or brunch right before a visit to the San Diego Zoo, which is close by.
1250 J St, San Diego. Tel: (619) 232 7662. Open: daily 7am–3pm.

The Prado £££
Lovely place for lunch on the outdoor patio, situated in Balboa Park. Very good kobe beef dishes.
1549 El Prado, San Diego. Tel: (619) 557 9441. www.cohnrestaurants.com.

Open: Mon–Fri 11.30am–3pm, Sat & Sun 11am–3pm, dinner Tue–Sun 5pm–late.

Palm Springs
Shanghai Red's Oyster Bar ££

Casual, energetic little restaurant with great fish tacos and fresh oysters. Located at the back of the Fisherman's Market & Grill.
235 S Indian Canyon Dr, Palm Springs.
Tel: (760) 322 9293.
www.fishermans.com.
Open: daily 4pm–late.

The Cowboy Way BBQ ££

Kansas City-style tender beef ribs, succulent pulled pork and other barbecued meats.
2000 N Palm Canyon Dr, Palm Springs.
Tel: (760) 325 8400. www. thecowboywaybbq.com.
Open: Mon–Thur 11am–8pm, Fri & Sat 11am–10pm, Sun noon–8pm.

Johnny Costa's Ristorante £££

Pizzas, pastas and tasty meatballs at this Italian restaurant.
440 S Palm Canyon Dr, Palm Springs. Tel: (760)

325 4556. www.johnny costaspalmsprings.com.
Open: Mon–Thur 5–9.30pm, Fri & Sat 5–10.30pm.

Palm Desert
French Corner Café ££

Desserts are the highlight of this casual diner – proper Parisian pastries that come in petit sizes too.
72423 Hwy 111, Palm Desert.
Tel: (760) 568 5362. www. frenchcornercafe.com.
Open: daily 8am–8pm.

CENTRAL CALIFORNIA
Santa Barbara
Lilly's Tacos £

Find cheap, fast and delicious pork tacos at this authentic hole-in-the-wall *taqueria*.
310 Chapala St, Santa Barbara. Tel: (805) 966 9180. www.lillystacos.com.
Open: Mon, Wed & Thur 11am–9pm, Fri & Sat 11am–10pm, Sun 11am–9.30pm.

Arigato Sushi £££

Inventive maki rolls such as the Yellow Submarine and the Pretty in Pink. Expensive but very fresh

fish in a hip, busy environment.
1225 State St, Santa Barbara.
Tel: (805) 965 6074. www. arigatosantabarbara.com.
Open: daily 5.30–10pm.

Bouchon £££

Romantic French restaurant. Try the blueberry cake for dessert, a local favourite.
9 W Victoria St, Santa Barbara. Tel: (805) 730 1160. www.bouchonsanta barbara.com. Open: Sun–Thur 5.30–9pm, Fri & Sat 5.30–10pm.

San Luis Obispo
House of Bread £

Fresh selection of baked pastries and breads. Try the cinnamon rolls and sandwiches.
299 Marsh St.
Tel: (805) 542 0255.
www.houseofbread.com.
Open: Mon–Fri 7am–7pm, Sat 7am–6.30pm, Sun 8am–5.30pm.

Jaffa Café £

Mediterranean food items including fresh pittas, falafel and baklava. Good value, nice family atmosphere.
1212 Higuera St, San Luis Obispo. Tel: (805) 543

2449. www.jaffacafe.us.
Open: Mon–Fri
10.30am–8pm, Sat & Sun
11am–8pm.

Big Sur
Deetjen's Restaurant £££
A bohemian restaurant
in Big Sur, with good
breakfasts and dinners in
a rustic arty setting.
48865 Hwy 1, Big Sur.
Tel: (831) 667 2378.
www.deetjens.com.
Open: daily for
breakfast and dinner
only, call for times and
reservations.

Carmel
Carmel Belle ££
Perfect for brunch, this
café, located inside a
shopping centre, has
some creative dishes
including green eggs &
ham and polenta with
truffled mushrooms.
Doud Craft Studios,
Ocean Ave & San Carlos,
Carmel.
Tel: (831) 624 1600.
www.carmelbelle.com.
Open: daily 8am–5pm.
Anton & Michel
Restaurant £££
Dress up for this French-
inspired Carmel
landmark, where

romance, history and
kobe beef short ribs make
for a lovely evening.
Mission St, between
Ocean Ave & 7th,
Carmel.
Tel: (831) 624 2406. www.
antonandmichel.com.
Open: daily 11.30am–
3pm & 5.30–9.30pm.

Monterey
Hula's Island Grill and
Tiki Room ££
Hawaiian-kitsch interior
with a range of dishes
including burgers, sushi
and tacos.
622 Lighthouse Ave,
Monterey.
Tel: (831) 655 4852.
www.hulastiki.com.
Open: Tue–Sat 11.30am–
2pm, Mon–Sun
4.30pm–late.
Lopez Restaurante y
Cantina ££
Family-owned,
traditional Mexican
restaurant with the
best chips & salsa
in town.
635 Cass St, Monterey.
Tel: (831) 324 4260.
www.
lopezrestaurante.com.
Open: Mon–Thur & Sun
11am–9pm, Fri & Sat
11am–10pm.

NORTHERN
CALIFORNIA
San Francisco
Buena Vista Café ££
Best Irish coffee around,
good breakfasts and
shared tables for those
feeling sociable.
2765 Hyde St, San
Francisco. Tel: (415) 474
5044. www.thebuenavista.
com. Open: Mon–Fri
9am–2am, Sat & Sun
8am–2am.
Café Gratitude ££
Vegetarian café with
organic, raw foods that
even carnivores
will enjoy.
2400 Harrison St,
San Francisco.
Tel: (415) 824 4652.
www.cafegratitude.com.
Open: daily 9am–10pm.
Fog City Diner ££
A yuppified diner
experience where the
menu features the likes
of oysters, crab cakes and
upmarket burgers.
1300 Battery St,
San Francisco.
Tel: (415) 982 2000.
www.fogcitydiner.com.
Open: Mon–Thur
11.30am–10pm, Fri
11.30am–11pm, Sat
10.30am–11pm, Sun
10.30am–10pm.

Delfina £££
Located in the hip part of the Mission District. Enjoy great pastas, pizzas and cheese plates.
3621 18th St, San Francisco. Tel: (415) 552 4055. www.delfinasf.com. Open: Mon–Thur 5.30–10pm, Fri & Sat 5.30–11pm, Sun 5–10pm.

Swan Oyster Depot £££
Located in affluent Nob Hill, this no-frills seafood specialist shop serves generous portions of clam chowder, crab salads and fresh raw oysters.
1517 Polk St, San Francisco. Tel: (415) 673 1101. Open: Mon–Sat 8am–5.30pm.

Wayfare Tavern £££
Popular new place cooking up classic American dishes.
558 Sacramento St, San Francisco. Tel: (415) 772 9060. www.wayfaretavern.com. Open: Mon–Fri 11.30am–11pm, Sat & Sun 5–11pm.

Chez Panisse ££££
Alice Waters' restaurant in Berkeley is still a gastronomic mecca. Book ahead.
1517 Shattuck Ave, Berkeley. Tel: (415) 548 5525. www.chezpanisse.com. Open: for dinner Mon–Sat from 6pm.

Fleur de Lys ££££
Hubert Keller is chef at this swanky French restaurant, whose fixed-price menu is as impressive as the décor.
777 Sutter St, San Francisco. Tel: (415) 673 7779. www.fleurdelyssf.com. Open: Tue–Thur 6–9.30pm, Fri 5.30–10.30pm, Sat 5–10.30pm.

Wine Country
Mustards Grill £££
Good option for lunch, with reasonable prices in comparison to most restaurants in the area.
7399 St Helena Hwy, Yountville. Tel: (707) 944 2424. www.mustardsgrill.com. Open: Mon–Thur 11.30am–9pm, Fri 11.30am–10pm, Sat 11am–10pm, Sun 11am–9pm.

Sacramento
Café Europa £
Inexpensive Greek restaurant with tasty sandwiches, located in an unimpressive strip mall.
1537 Howe Ave, Suite 116, Sacramento. Tel: (916) 779 0737. Open: Mon–Sat 11am–8.30pm.

Tower Café ££
Fantastic French toast and other brunch items.
1518 Broadway, Sacramento. Tel: (916) 441 0222. www.towercafe.com. Open: Mon–Thur 8am–11pm, Fri & Sat 8am–midnight.

Gold Country
Sierra Nevada Taproom and Restaurant ££
Popular spot so get there early. Good pub-style food; try the beer sampler.
1075 E 20th St, Chico. Tel: (530) 345 2739. www.sierranevada.com. Open: Sun–Thur 11am–9pm, Fri & Sat 11am–10pm.

Lake Tahoe and environs
Fire Sign Café ££
Local breakfast spot with big, hearty portions. Try their home-baked cobblers.
1785 W Lake Blvd, Tahoe City. Tel: (530) 583 0871. Open: daily 7am–3pm.

Accommodation

California has an enormous choice of accommodation, from budget to super-luxury, and it is all comparatively inexpensive compared with much of the rest of the world. It is also of an almost universally high standard. Even the cheapest places are clean and well appointed. This does not include inner-city residential hotels that cater for transients and often look as though they went out of business decades ago.

TYPES OF ACCOMMODATION

Hostels

Very low-cost accommodation ($20–30 per night) is available in both YMCA/YWCA hostels (known as 'Y') or in Youth Hostels (AYH) (*www.ymca.net* and *www.hiusa.org*).

Motels

The motel, of course, is the American lodging par excellence. For the budget-conscious traveller, these are by far the best places to stay. They can be unbelievably cheap and provide a clean, simply decorated room, usually with the choice of double, queen- or king-sized beds. There is always a television, telephone and en-suite bathroom.

Motels tend to be on the outskirts of town on the main roads and are rarely in the best locations for sightseeing. If you have a car this is not a problem. Motels are usually well advertised with huge roadside signs. Most towns have a motel strip; in San Francisco it is Lombard Street.

Breakfast is sometimes offered in the lobby, but, if not, there is usually a restaurant close by and vending machines for soft drinks.

Hotels

Full-service hotels are much more expensive than motels and are usually well located near main tourist attractions.

Bed and breakfasts

Northern California has a growing number of bed and breakfast inns. Do not be deceived: these are not the budget seaside accommodations of Europe, with rates of $100–250 per night. In California they can be more expensive than some hotels. The Victorian motif of most places is a big selling point with Californians who are hungry for history, however recent. For further information, contact the **California Association of Bed & Breakfast Inns** (*tel: (800) 373 9251; www.cabbi.com*).

Staying in style

California has some of the great classic hotels of the world for those who can afford them (upwards of $200, but anything up to several thousand dollars for a suite per night). Even in hotels of this quality breakfast is rarely included in the price.

Once you have checked into one of these luxury resorts there is no reason to set foot in the outside world again until your money runs out.

Getting the best value

There are several ways to ensure you get the lowest rate possible. It's worth trying websites such as Expedia, Hotwire and Priceline, as well as the hotel's own website, which may offer special deals. If reserving by phone, try calling the hotel's front desk rather than a general reservation number. Always ask about reductions, especially if you're travelling off season.

Long-distance calls from in-room telephones can be marked up by quite outrageous amounts, and it's wise to avoid in-room minibars.

WHERE TO STAY

The following key is an indication of accommodation price. The £ sign indicates the approximate cost per standard room, per night, based on double occupancy during peak season.

£	under $100
££	$100–150
£££	$150–200
££££	over $200

Beverly Wilshire Hotel, Beverly Hills

Accommodation

SOUTHERN CALIFORNIA
Los Angeles
The Cadillac Hotel ££

A no-frills, comfortable hotel located directly on the famous Venice Beach boardwalk. Good value for a great location if exploring Venice and Santa Monica.
8 Dudley Ave, Venice.
Tel: (310) 399 8876.
www.thecadillachotel.com

Candy Cane Inn ££

A 10-minute walk to Disneyland®, affordable pricing and complimentary breakfast. Perfect for a family visit to the area's attractions, includes shuttle services and free parking.
1747 S Harbor Blvd, Anaheim.
Tel: (714) 774 5284.
www.candycaneinn.net

Hollywood Heights Hotel ££

Contemporary, boutique-style hotel in a central location that is within walking distance of many tourist attractions.
2005 N Highland Ave, Hollywood.
Tel: (323) 876 8600.
www.hollywoodheights hotel.com

Magic Castle Hotel £££

As the name suggests, this castle-like hotel is in a central location for various tourist attractions and offers spacious rooms with friendly service.
7025 Franklin Ave, Hollywood.
Tel: (800) 741 4915.
www.magiccastlehotel.com

The Beverly Hills Hotel and Bungalows ££££

Famous landmark hotel that continues to attract notables. Set in a central location with tennis courts and a spa on site. New for 2011 are the 'ultra bungalows', which are a luxury home away from home featuring a private plunge pool, fitness equipment, fireplaces and all the other requirements of an LA celebrity.
9641 Sunset Blvd, Beverly Hills. Tel: (310) 276 2251.
www.beverlyhillshotel.com

Hotel Bel Air ££££

An LA classic, with private-entrance rooms appointed with fine Italian linen, fireplaces and luxury bath amenities. Currently undergoing an extensive renovation that includes a new spa and additional suites. The Hotel Bel Air will reopen in the summer of 2011.
701 Stone Canyon Rd, Bel Air. Tel: (310) 472 1211.
www.hotelbelair.com

San Diego
The Elsbree House ££

Half a block from the coast, this relaxing B&B fits right into the laid-back, friendly surfer atmosphere of Ocean Beach.
5054 Narragansett Ave, San Diego. Tel: (619) 226 4133. www.bbinnob.com

Keating House ££

Elegant Victorian B&B with a lush garden, located within walking distance of Balboa Park, San Diego Zoo and downtown. Free Wi-Fi and an excellent breakfast is provided.
2331 2nd Ave, San Diego.
Tel: (800) 995 8644.
www.keatinghouse.com

Hotel Solamar £££

Suave, vibrant hotel right in the heart of downtown San Diego in the Gaslamp District, with plenty of restaurants and bars only steps away.

435 6th Ave, San Diego.
Tel: (619) 819 9500.
www.hotelsolamar.com

Tower23 Hotel £££

Great location on the
beach with urban, ultra-
modern designs
throughout the hotel.
4551 Ocean Blvd, San
Diego. Tel: (858) 270
2323. www.t23hotel.com

Hotel del Coronado ££££

Built in 1888, this grand
Victorian marvel is
beautifully situated on a
wide stretch of beach and
has modern, roomy
suites. A good restaurant
is on site too.
1500 Orange Ave,
Coronado.
Tel: (800) 468 3533.
www.hoteldel.com

Anza-Borrego Desert State Park

Borrego Valley Inn £££

Rustic desert
surroundings, warm
Santa Fe architecture and
a chance to swim under
the night sky in one of
two pools, one of which
is clothing optional. No
restaurant on site but the
inn does provide
breakfast.
405 Palm Canyon Dr,
Borrego Springs.

Tel: (760) 767 0311. www.
borregovalleyinn.com

Death Valley

Amargosa Opera House and Hotel ££

An eccentric experience
in a ghost town, with
basic, comfortable rooms
that used to house borax
miners in the 1920s.
608 Hwy 127, Death
Valley Junction.
Tel: (760) 852 4441.
www.amargosa-opera-
house.com

Furnace Creek Resort ££££

As accommodations are
limited in Death Valley
National Park, this resort
is a welcome but
expensive oasis located
near many of the major
park sights. Closed from
May to Oct.
Hwy 190, Death Valley
National Park.
Tel: (760) 786 2345. www.
furnacecreekresort.com

Joshua Tree National Park

Desert Lily ££

Located just outside
Joshua Tree National Park,
this B&B has pleasant
guest rooms, each with a
private bathroom.

Desert Lily St, Joshua
Tree. Tel: (760) 366 4676.
www.thedesertlily.com

Palm Springs

Caliente Tropics Hotel £

Tiki-style hotel from the
1960s, with modern,
clean rooms, pet friendly,
and a nice large pool that
Elvis once enjoyed.
411 E Palm Canyon Dr,
Palm Springs.
Tel: (760) 327 1391.
www.calientetropics.com

Andreas Hotel & Spa £££

Attractive, stone
Spanish Revival hotel
from the 1930s.
Downtown location
with modern, luxury
rooms and relaxing spa
services.
227 N Indian Canyon Dr,
Palm Springs.
Tel: (760) 327 5701.
www.andreashotel.com

El Morocco Inn & Spa £££

Find arched doorways
and billowing fabrics at
this 1940s-era French-
Moroccan retreat in the
desert. Perfect for a
romantic getaway.
66810 4th St,
Desert Hot Springs.
Tel: (760) 288 2527.
www.elmoroccoinn.com

Ace Hotel & Swim Club ££££

Boutique hotel and resort with contemporary, bohemian rooms. Some are dog friendly, and some have vinyl record players, fireplaces and fun retro furniture. Pool, spa, gym, restaurant and even a snow cone vendor on site.
701 E Palm Canyon Dr, Palm Springs.
Tel: (760) 325 9900.
www.acehotel.com

CENTRAL CALIFORNIA
Santa Barbara
The Presidio Motel ££
Modern, inexpensive motel in a good location with free Wi-Fi, continental breakfast and complimentary cruiser bikes to explore downtown Santa Barbara.
1620 State St, Santa Barbara.
Tel: (805) 963 1355. www. thepresidiomotel.com

San Ysidro Ranch ££££
Decadent, 5-star luxury at this California ranch, with beautiful mountainous surroundings.
900 San Ysidro Ln, Santa Barbara.
Tel: (805) 565 1700.
www.sanysidroranch.com

The Upham Hotel & Country House ££££
Classic country hideaway from 1871 and the oldest continuously operating hotel in the state.
1404 De La Vina St, Santa Barbara.
Tel: (800) 727 0876.
www.uphamhotel.com

San Luis Obispo
Madonna Inn £££
This quirky roadside icon has been offering themed accommodations for over 50 years. Choose from such rooms as the Caveman, Safari or Krazy Dazy.
100 Madonna Rd, San Luis Obispo.
Tel: (805) 543 3000.
www.madonnainn.com

San Simeon
Sands by the Sea Motel £
Clean, reasonably priced rooms. Beach access and minutes from the popular Hearst Castle.
9355 Hearst Dr, San Simeon. Tel: (800) 444 0779. www.sandsmotel.com

Big Sur
Post Ranch Inn £££
An exclusive cabin resort high on a cliff, with finely appointed rooms that feature beautiful ocean and forest views. Wonderful restaurant on site.
Hwy 1, Big Sur.
Tel: (888) 524 4787.
www.postranchinn.com

Ripplewood Resort £££
Rustic cabins surrounded by giant redwoods, located right along the Big Sur River.
47047 Hwy 1, Big Sur.
Tel: (831) 667 2242. www. ripplewoodresort.com

TreeBones Resort £££
Camp in style at this ocean-view resort where accommodation is in peaceful yurts. Regular campsites are also available, as is the Human Nest, a uniquely designed wood-woven nest that has room for two sleeping bags and pillows.
71895 Hwy 1, Big Sur.
Tel: (877) 424 4787.
www.treebonesresort.com

Carmel
Mission Ranch £££
Once a dairy farm from the 1850s, this historic property, complete with grazing sheep, was renovated by former Carmel Mayor, Clint

Eastwood. Choice of rooms in the main farmhouse or private cottages and barns.
26270 Dolores St, Carmel.
Tel: (831) 624 6436. www. missionranchcarmel.com

The Lodge at Pebble Beach ££££
Top-notch resort for serious golf enthusiasts. Most of the guest rooms have wood-burning fireplaces and incredible ocean views.
1700 17-Mile Dr,
Pebble Beach.
Tel: (800) 654 9300.
www.pebblebeach.com

Monterey
Monterey Plaza Hotel & Spa ££££
Well-established hotel in a central location on the bay with sophisticated rooms and notable restaurants on site.
400 Cannery Row,
Monterey.
Tel: (831) 646 1700. www. montereyplazahotel.com

Sequoia and Kings Canyon National Parks
Sequoia River Dance B&B ££
Warm and inviting B&B just outside Sequoia

National Park, with the property backing on to the Kaweah River.
40534 Cherokee Oaks Dr,
Three Rivers.
Tel: (559) 561 4411. www. sequoiariverdance.com

The Wuksachi Lodge ££££
Ideally situated in the heart of Sequoia National Park. Pricey room rates include breakfast.
64740 Wuksachi Way,
Sequoia National Park.
Tel: (866) 807 3598.
www.visitsequoia.com

NORTHERN CALIFORNIA
San Francisco
Chancellor Hotel ££
Classic boutique hotel at Union Square, right on the cable-car line to Fisherman's Wharf. Plenty of free extras such as Wi-Fi, snacks in the lobby and a pillow menu.
433 Powell St,
San Francisco.
Tel: (415) 362 2004.
www.chancellorhotel.com

Golden Gate Hotel ££
Charming B&B in prestigious Nob Hill. All 25 rooms are beautifully decorated and there is

free Wi-Fi throughout.
775 Bush St,
San Francisco.
Tel: (415) 392 3702.
www.goldengatehotel.com

Argonaut Hotel £££
Nautically inspired, boutique waterfront hotel at Fisherman's Wharf. Pleasant, spacious rooms with quality amenities.
495 Jefferson St,
San Francisco.
Tel: (415) 563 0800.
www.argonauthotel.com

Hotel Bohème £££
Arty boutique hotel in North Beach with a Beat-era flavour. Intimate guest rooms come with free Wi-Fi.
444 Columbus Ave,
San Francisco.
Tel: (415) 433 9111.
www.hotelboheme.com

Hotel Shattuck Plaza £££
Recently renovated upmarket boutique hotel in downtown Berkeley that has still retained its old-world charm.
2086 Allston Way, Berkeley.
Tel: (510) 845 7300. www. hotelshattuckplaza.com

The Orchard Garden Hotel ££££
This is one of San Francisco's most eco-friendly hotels without

compromising on comfort and style.
466 Bush St,
San Francisco.
Tel: (415) 399 9807. www.
theorchardgardenhotel.com

Wine Country
Auberge du Soleil ££££
Overlooking the valley below, this high-end romantic resort includes a world-renowned spa with fabulous, restorative treatments and a Michelin-star-rated restaurant.
180 Rutherford Hill Rd,
Rutherford.
Tel: (707) 963 1211.
www.aubergedusoleil.com

Calistoga Ranch ££££
Lavish resort featuring private guest lodges with fireplaces and en-suite outdoor showers.
580 Lommel Rd,
Calistoga.
Tel: (707) 254 2800.
www.calistogaranch.com

Sacramento
Delta King Hotel ££
Permanently docked authentic riverboat with clean and tidy accommodation and a good restaurant on board.
1000 Front St,
Sacramento.
Tel: (916) 444 5464.
www.deltaking.com

The Citizen Hotel ££££
Downtown luxury with a historic flair and within walking distance of many major sites in the city including the Capitol building, Old Town, various museums and the Convention Center. The Grange restaurant at the Citizen is excellent, and there are more restaurants and shops nearby.
926 J St, Sacramento.
Tel: (916) 447 2700.
www.citizenhotel.com

Gold Country
1859 Historic National Hotel ££
This hotel has been in continuous operation since its first opening days during the Gold Rush era. Rooms are quaint, with period antiques, and the bar downstairs has plenty of stories to tell. Try the private soaker tub while listening out for ghosts.
18183 Main St,
Jamestown.
Tel: (800) 894 3446.
www.national-hotel.com

Gate House Inn £££
Traditional Victorian Inn with pretty guest rooms in the main house and also a private cottage at the back of the property. Enjoy generous breakfasts on the porch, and there's also an outdoor swimming pool. Close to downtown Jackson and Sutter Creek.
1330 Jackson Gate Rd,
Jackson.
Tel: (209) 223 3500.
www.gatehouseinn.com

Lake Tahoe and environs
968 Hotel £££
Conveniently located and endeavours to be an environmentally friendly hotel with features such as organic sheets and toiletries, and reclaimed wooden details. Parking and Internet are included, and the Gondola ride is only minutes away.
968 Park Ave, South Lake Tahoe.
Tel: (877) 544 0968.
www.968parkhotel.com

Cedar Glen Lodge £££
Cosy cabins with complimentary breakfast and Wi-Fi. Located across the street from

Accommodation

the famous blue lake.
*6589 N Lake Blvd, Tahoe
Vista. Tel: (530) 546 4281.
www.tahoecedarglen.com*

The High Sierra

**Highland House Bed &
Breakfast Inn ££**
Secluded, three-
guestroom home set
among four forested
hectares (10 acres), just
outside Yosemite National
Park. Delicious breakfasts
and Wi-Fi included.
*3125 Wild Dove Ln,
Mariposa.
Tel: (209) 966 3737. www.
highlandhouseinn.com*

Château du Sureau ££££
European elegance and
opulence at this inn near
the southern entrance to

Yosemite National Park.
*48688 Victoria Ln,
Oakhurst.
Tel: (559) 683 6860.
www.chateausureau.com*

The north coast

Lighthouse Inn £
Standard, clean rooms
with all the usual
amenities.
*681 Hwy 101,
Crescent City.
Tel: (877) 464 3993. www.
crescentcitylighthouseinn.
com*

**The North Cliff
Hotel £££**
Splendid
accommodation with
ocean-view spa tubs, gas
fireplaces and romantic
balconies.

*1005 S Main St, Fort
Bragg.
Tel: (866) 962 2550.
www.northcliffhotel.net*

**The Stanford Inn by the
Sea ££££**
Overlooking Mendocino
Bay, this inn has all the
ingredients for a relaxing
weekend getaway. Guest
rooms have wood-
burning fireplaces, free
Wi-Fi and healthy
breakfasts. The property
amenities include an
indoor swimming pool,
bike and canoe rentals
and an organic garden.
Pets are very welcome.
*Hwy 1 and Comptche
Ukiah Rd, Mendocino.
Tel: (707) 937 5615.
www.stanfordinn.com*

The Hilton in Beverly Hills

Practical guide

Arriving

Documents

All travellers to the US must have a machine-readable or e-passport that is valid for at least 90 days from their date of entry into the US. Citizens of many countries, including the UK, Ireland, Australia and New Zealand, do not need a visa for stays of less than 90 days but must have a return ticket (or open standby) and an address for at least their first night's accommodation in the US (or proof of a fly-drive itinerary). Citizens from these countries will be given a customs form and a visa waiver form by their airline, which should be filled out before arrival and handed in at immigration (note that the queues are often long and sometimes take an hour or more to clear). However, it is always best to check this information well before you travel: contact your nearest US consulate or embassy: *www.usembassy.gov*

Note that you should always carry photo ID when travelling around the US, especially if you are hiring a car, or if you are planning on buying alcohol.

By air

Los Angeles International (LAX) is the main airport for international flights into southern California, handling over 60 airlines; San Diego is smaller and it is used by some international charter companies. San Francisco International serves northern California, with Oakland and San Jose handling some charter flights.

Domestic flights are generally very expensive, with the exception of the services between San Francisco and Los Angeles. If planning short hops within the state or flying in from another state, it is advisable to purchase a ticket before arrival. Several airlines offer air passes, and travel agents should be able to advise on the best deals.

Virtually all California's commercial airports have all the facilities a traveller would expect, although only the major airports will have banking facilities. Travellers with disabilities are usually well provided for. Services available for business travellers include conference rooms and a wide range of communications facilities.

At both Los Angeles International and San Francisco International there is a wide range of choice for transport into town. There are several taxis, buses and car rental companies. Airporters offer a door-to-door service for much less than a taxi but take longer as they carry other passengers and make frequent stops. Most major hotels in the vicinity offer a free shuttle service.

Major airlines

Air Canada *Tel: (888) 247 2262.*
www.aircanada.com
Air New Zealand *Tel: (800) 028 4149.*
www.airnewzealand.com

American Airlines *Tel: (800) 433 7300. www.aa.com*
British Airways *Tel: (800) 247 9297. www.britishairways.com*
Continental Airlines *Tel: (800) 523 3273 domestic/(800) 231 0856 international. www.continental.com*
Delta Airlines *Tel: (800) 221 1212 domestic/(800) 241 4141 international. www.delta.com*
Frontier *Tel: (800) 432 1359. www.frontierairlines.com*
Jetblue *Tel: (800) 538 2583. www.jetblue.com*
Qantas *Tel: (800) 227 4500. www.qantas.com.au*
Southwest *Tel: (800) 435 9792. www.southwest.com*
United Airlines *Tel: (800) 864 8331 domestic/(800) 538 2929 international. www.united.com*
US Airways *Tel: (800) 428 4322. www.usairways.com*
Virgin Atlantic *Tel: (800) 821 5438. www.virgin-atlantic.com*
(All these numbers are toll-free.)

Camping

The Californian climate lends itself to camping holidays and outside the major cities there is no shortage of campsites.

Campsites are found in parks throughout California, and are managed by a variety of agencies. California State Parks controls state park lands, the National Park Service covers national park lands, and the US Forest Service is in charge of national forest lands. In addition, there are private companies such as Kampgrounds of America (KOA) and Thousand Trails.

Facilities vary from site to site: those run by private companies tend to have more amenities, such as proper showers and even Wi-Fi, but they usually charge higher prices; the most basic campsites are generally those found in national parks and forests. Campsites, especially in popular parks such as Yosemite, get booked up months in advance, so it's always best to reserve as far ahead as possible.

In some parks, you are also allowed to camp in the back country but you may need a Wilderness Pass.

Bears can be a serious problem at many campsites, and there are strict rules concerning storage of food. Never ignore the warnings and rules laid down by the park service.

For more information and to make reservations, contact:
California State Parks and US Forest Service *Tel: (800) 444 7275* or visit *www.reserveamerica.com* for reservations; visit *www.parks.ca.gov* and *www.fs.fed.us* for information.
National Park Service *Tel: (877) 444 6777* or visit *www.recreation.gov* for reservations; visit *www.nps.gov* for information.
KOA *Tel: (888) 562 0000. www.koa.com*
Thousand Trails *Tel: (800) 205 0606. www.thousandtrails.com*

On-site tent hire is not generally available, but equipment can be bought inexpensively from sports shops. Camper vans are available for hire in major towns. In the US they are called motor homes and they are not available from regular car hire sources. One of the biggest companies is **Cruise America** (*tel: (800) 671 8042 toll-free; www.cruiseamerica.com*).

Children

Throughout the state children are well catered for. Many hotels provide cots (cribs) at no extra charge, and extra beds for older children are available at a nominal charge. Larger hotels offer babysitting services that are safe and reliable. Many restaurants have children's menus or offer children's portions from the main

menu. High chairs are universally available. Food and nappies (diapers) for infants are available in profusion at any supermarket or drugstore, and in most towns they will be available 24 hours a day from at least one convenience store. Baby milk is called formula and is available in several dairy and non-dairy varieties. California is generally safe for tourists, but never leave children unattended.

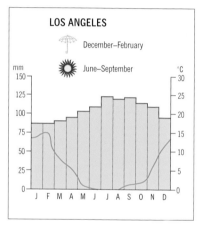

WEATHER CONVERSION CHART

25.4mm = 1 inch

$°F = 1.8 × °C + 32$

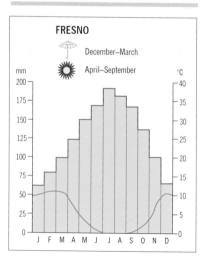

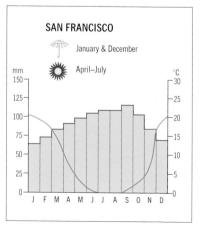

Climate

The best months for travel are generally April to June and September to November. In July and August the temperatures can be sizzling in the deserts of southern California and cold and foggy on the north coast and in San Francisco. December to March has the most rainfall, although southern California has recently suffered from droughts. During these months, the snowfall in the high Sierra provides world-class skiing, and when it stops snowing the skies are usually blue. Winter is the best time to visit the deserts, and in March the flowers will be starting to bloom.

Consulate Generals

Australia *575 Market St, Suite 1800, 18th Floor, San Francisco, CA 94105. Tel: (415) 644 3620. www.dfat.gov.au*
Canada *550 S Hope St, Los Angeles, CA 90071. Tel: (213) 346 2700. www.canadainternational.gc.ca*
Ireland *100 Pine St, 33rd Floor, San Francisco, CA 94111. Tel: (415) 392 4214.*
New Zealand *2425 Olympic Blvd, Suite 600E, Santa Monica, CA 90404. Tel: (310) 566 6555. www.nzcgla.com*
United Kingdom *11766 Wilshire Blvd, Suite 1200, Los Angeles, CA 90025. Tel: (310) 481 0031. www.fco.gov.uk*
1 Sansome St, Suite 850, San Francisco, CA 94104. Tel: (415) 617 1300.

Crime

Crime is a very real problem but should be put into perspective. It is at its worst in the big cities but not really any worse than in many other major cities throughout the world.

General availability of handguns is one of the major problems, but the chances of even seeing a gun, other than on a policeman's hip, are very remote. Most shootings are in areas that tourists would rarely visit. However, it is unwise to get into a confrontational situation with anyone, particularly while driving. Frayed tempers have often been known to result in shootings. It is also unwise to pick up hitchhikers (and illegal to do so on freeways).

A more real problem is theft, from both cars and hotel rooms. Take sensible precautions and make sure valuables are not openly on display. Most hotel thefts are opportunist, and the more difficult it is to snatch something and run the less chance it will be stolen.

Some people prefer to carry traveller's cheques rather than cash. All hotels and most shops and restaurants will accept US dollar cheques, which can be purchased before leaving home. Thomas Cook, VISA and American Express traveller's cheques are widely recognised and provide fast service in the case of loss or theft.

Shopping is usually trouble-free. Prices for consumer goods in the US are generally much lower than in other parts of the world, but care should be taken in some tourist areas, particularly with cameras and electronic goods. Buy an appropriate magazine and look at the small ads in the back. You may not be able to equal the prices you find there, which are often for New York stores, but it will give you a good idea of the general range.

Protection can be obtained if you pay by credit card. If the goods are unsatisfactory the charge can often be disputed with the credit card company.

Customs regulations

Everyone entering the US must pass through US customs. Personal allowances for visitors include one litre of spirits or wine, 200 cigarettes or 50 cigars, plus up to $100 worth of gifts. In practice, most of these items are far cheaper within the US than at airport duty-free shops.

There is no restriction on the amount of currency imported or exported, but anything over $10,000 must be declared.

US customs are particularly concerned about drugs, animals, meat (both fresh and processed), plants and fresh fruit. Penalties are severe.

Driving
Accidents

1. Set up warning signs. Flares are usually used in California and are available from any auto store.
2. Call police and an ambulance if required. The emergency telephone number is *911*.
3. Take the names and addresses of all involved, the licence plates of the other vehicle(s), and the names and numbers of insurance policies.
4. Write down names and addresses of any witnesses, together with the time and date of the accident. If possible, take photographs of the accident from several angles.
5. Under no circumstance admit to or sign any statement of responsibility.

Breakdown

The American Automobile Association (AAA, or Triple A), which offers roadside assistance to its US members, is affiliated with clubs such as the AA in Britain and provides services such as free maps and guides to foreign visitors. For more information, including a list of AAA offices in California, visit *www.calif.aaa.com*

Car hire

Every airport, however small, will have at least one car rental company associated with it. The major airports have several. All the major companies are represented (Hertz, Avis, Budget, National and Dollar), but there are hundreds of local companies that often offer better rates. Generally, off-airport companies offer the best value and they all provide a free shuttle service to their facility.

It is usually better to arrange for a car before arriving. Several airlines have special deals available with preferential rates if the booking is made in advance. It is always better to make a reservation if possible, as certain categories of car may be in short supply during peak seasons.

Automatic transmission is standard on all rental cars. American cars are big and a so-called mid-size is huge by European standards. The smallest size available is the sub-compact, which will carry just four people and a small amount of luggage. For summer travel, ask for a car with air conditioning. It should be available at no extra cost.

None of the major car rental companies will rent to anyone under the age of 25. It may be possible to find a local company that will, but be prepared to pay a loaded insurance premium.

Extra insurances such as liability insurance (SLI) and collision damage waiver (CDW) are vital, although they can be almost 50 per cent of the rental fee. You may already be covered by your own personal car insurance policy. Check before leaving home.

In cases of breakdown, immediately call the car rental company and await instructions.

Documentation

Drivers will need a valid driver's licence from their home country (and a passport if travelling with a non-photo licence).

Driving tips

In America, driving is on the right-hand side of the road. At first, the number of lanes on motorways (freeways) can be offputting to non-US drivers, especially as exit lanes frequently peel off to the right, but once you get used to that it's pretty straightforward. Traffic, however, can get very solid in and around major cities, in particular Los Angeles and San Francisco, so allow plenty of time for journeys. Using smaller roads may not buy you much time because there are so many traffic lights.

The view from the Coit Tower in San Francisco highlights the straight roads in the city

Major roads are well maintained and well signposted, although it's often worth spending the extra on a GPS navigation system in your rental car to save yourself from getting lost.

You can make a right turn at a red traffic light unless a sign says otherwise.

Parking

Parking spaces can be hard to find in major cities and popular tourist towns such as Carmel, although meters (which take 25 cent coins) are much cheaper than in the UK. Look out for restrictions, which are usually also written on nearby signs (note that a red kerb means no parking at any time). Parking garages are plentiful, although they cost more.

Petrol

California is a car-oriented state and there is no shortage of petrol stations and garage facilities. Petrol, called gas,

'Cable car' tour of downtown San Francisco

is available in 87, 89 and 91 octane. Diesel is also available at most petrol stations.

All petrol stations have good maps for sale, and most car rental companies will have local maps available free of charge.

Speed limits

Inter-city motorways are called freeways and other roads are highways. The speed limit on most highways and freeways is 105km/h (65mph) unless otherwise posted. In most towns the limit is between 40 and 56km/h (25 and 35mph). Speed limits are strictly enforced. On freeways you can theoretically be ticketed for driving too slowly in the left hand lane, but this rarely happens.

For more details on Driving and Parking see pp21–3.

Electricity

The standard supply is 110 volts at 60 cycles. Adaptors are readily available for purchase in the US, but it may be easier to bring one from home to save time finding a shop that sells them.

Emergency telephone numbers

Police, **Fire** and **Ambulance** *911.*

Health

There are no specific health requirements for visitors to California. The standard of healthcare is extremely high, but so are the costs, and it is essential to have a good insurance policy. Many doctors and hospitals will refuse to give treatment unless proof of insurance can be given. All major hospitals have 24-hour emergency rooms.

Information on doctors can be obtained from hotels or online. California does not have many specific health problems. Tap water is drinkable but, if hiking, do not drink water from the streams, as it often carries the parasite Giardia.

AIDS is a continuing concern, particularly in the San Francisco area. The California AIDS Hotline telephone number is *(415) 863 2437*. Needless to say, safe sex is an absolute necessity.

Insurance

Travel insurance to cover both loss of property and medical expenses is highly recommended. Make sure that medical policies give adequate cover, including emergency flights home. Cancellation insurance is advisable if appropriate.

Internet

Increasing numbers of hotels, coffee shops and so on have Wi-Fi Internet access. Sometimes it is free, but sometimes you have to pay. Frequent travellers might want to subscribe to Boingo (*www.boingo.com*), which provides access to a wide range of Wi-Fi hotspots for a low fee. Free Wi-Fi is available in an increasing number of public areas, in particular in the Bay Area and Wine Country.

CONVERSION TABLE

FROM	TO	MULTIPLY BY
Inches	Centimetres	2.54
Feet	Metres	0.3048
Yards	Metres	0.9144
Miles	Kilometres	1.6090
Acres	Hectares	0.4047
Gallons	Litres	4.5460
Ounces	Grams	28.35
Pounds	Grams	453.6
Pounds	Kilograms	0.4536
Tons	Tonnes	1.0160

To convert back, for example from centimetres to inches, divide by the number in the third column.

Laundry

All major hotels have one-day laundry and dry-cleaning services from Monday to Friday. Alternatively, there are many dry-cleaning shops offering a two- to four-hour service.

Maps

General maps are available from car hire companies. More detailed town maps and walking maps are usually available free of charge at Chambers of Commerce or Visitor Bureaux. Detailed trekking maps are on sale at the National Park Visitor Centres.

Measurement and sizes

California still uses the imperial system of measurement.

Media

The closest there is to a national daily newspaper in California is the *Los Angeles Times*. In northern California the *San Francisco Chronicle* is the major daily, but it tends to be rather parochial. In most towns you can find both the *Wall Street Journal* and the *New York Times*, which often give a more global view of the news.

For local news, including weather and traffic conditions, keep the car radio tuned to one of the news stations. There is a radio station for virtually every interest from classical to rap, and there is also what is known as 'talk radio', which attracts calls from the fringes of society and is usually banal at best. It can, however, provide an amusing diversion and an insight into the American psyche.

In most parts of the state it is possible to receive a public radio station. The quality of programming is considerably more intelligent than the other networks and they carry the BBC News. Visit *www.npr.org* to find one.

Virtually every hotel and motel room in the state will have a television. More often than not, it will be cable TV offering 30 or more channels. The problem is finding one worth watching. As with radio, there are usually two or three Public Broadcasting Service (PBS) stations that give good news coverage, even if most of the other programmes are second-hand from British TV.

The newspapers all carry full TV guides, but there are no radio listings and you just have to keep trying until you find a station you like. For an online list, visit *www.officialusa.com*

Money matters

Banking hours have traditionally been 10am–3pm Monday to Friday, but recent competition has resulted in longer opening hours and even Saturday opening. There is no longer a general rule, except that the 10–3 core period is the same.

Smaller banks may not offer foreign exchange facilities, but it is possible to exchange money at the airport or hotel. You can withdraw money from cash machines (ATMs) using your credit or debit card, as long as you know your PIN. A charge will be levied by both your home bank and the US one.

It is useful to have small-denomination cheques when using them as cash.

The US dollar bill is available in denominations of 1, 5, 10, 20, 50 and 100. Be very careful, as all notes are exactly the same size and vary only slightly in colour. It is better to avoid the higher denomination to avoid expensive mistakes. Coins come in denominations of 1 cent (penny), 5 (nickel), 10 (dime) and 25 (quarter). Always keep a few quarters handy for parking meters and newspapers.

All major credit cards are universally accepted.

Sales tax is applied to all goods and restaurant meals within California. An additional 8.25–10.75 per cent (depending upon the county) will be added to the price tag.

Hotel taxes vary, but can be as much as 17 per cent.

National and state holidays

1 January New Year's Day
January, 3rd Mon Martin Luther King, Jr Day
February, 3rd Mon President's Day
May, last Mon Memorial Day
4 July Independence Day
September, 1st Mon Labor Day
October, 2nd Mon Columbus Day
11 November Veterans Day
November, 4th Thur Thanksgiving
25 December Christmas Day

Government offices, including post offices as well as some museums, are closed for most of these holidays. Shops remain open on all but Thanksgiving and Christmas. Peak periods for travel, hotels and campsites are Memorial Day, Independence Day and Labor Day. Air travel peaks at Thanksgiving and Christmas.

Opening hours

Most larger shops are open seven days a week, typically from 10am to 6pm and from noon on Sundays. Smaller shops and businesses close on Sundays.

Most offices open Monday to Friday, 9am–5pm.

Museums and art gallery timings vary dramatically. Many major galleries and museums open late on at least one night of the week, and close on one day (often Monday).

Organised tours

The majority of people visiting California hire cars, which is undoubtedly the best way to see the state. If time is limited a tour may be the best solution. Particularly in cities, tours can remove the headache of searching for parking spaces, and will also ensure that all the major sites are covered.

There are both regular and specialised tours available in the three major cities. If time is limited, a regular tour may fit the bill, but it will be with a large busload of tourists on a fairly superficial trip. The specialised tours cater for specific interests and are usually with smaller groups of people.

Dozens of tour operators serve California, and hotels will usually be able to give advice on what is available.

Regular tours of Los Angeles are given by **LA Sightseeing Tours**. **Tower Tours** operate in San Francisco, and in San Diego **San Diego Scenic Tours** offer 4-hour tours of the city.
Los Angeles *Tel: (800) 870 1886. www.lasightseeing.net*
San Francisco *Tel: (866) 345 8687. www.towertours.com*
San Diego *Tel: (858) 273 8687. www.sandiegoscenictours.com*

Specialised tours

Cable Car Charters motorised 'cable cars' pick up passengers every day from 11am from Fisherman's Wharf in San Francisco for a two-hour tour of the city, including the Golden Gate Bridge. The tour is very basic but the transportation is interesting (*tel: 415 596 9929. www.classiccablecar.com*).

For more adventurous visitors, LA Gang Tours offers two-hour informative bus tours through South Central Los Angeles with proceeds going towards improving this inner-city region. Scheduled stops include a visit to a local county jail, a detention centre, a graffiti art gallery and various real-life gang neighbourhoods (*tel: 213 265 4950. www.lagangtours.com*).

Pharmacies

Most pharmacies are open from at least 9am until 6pm, and many have longer hours. Drugstores usually have a pharmacy counter for dispensing prescriptions, and these are often open until 9pm. Some drugstores and pharmacies are open 24 hours. Major chains include **Rite Aid** and **Walgreens**.

Many non-prescription drugs can be obtained from regular supermarkets.

Places of worship

California is known to be home to various unconventional forms of worship. Cults, sects and alternative religions appear to flourish in the state as much as the more conventional churches and temples. While the Catholic Church has the largest following, California is also home to the largest Muslim population in the US.

Los Angeles has the second-largest Jewish community in the country, and there are many beautiful synagogues, Buddhist temples, Islamic mosques and a range of more unusual shrines to be seen throughout. Local newspapers generally list times of services for the main denominations.

Police

Every incorporated city in California has its own police force with normal police responsibilities, including traffic control. An incorporated city can have a population as small as 500, though the average is 2,300.

The areas outside the cities are policed by the county sheriff, a different title but essentially the same job except that they have no jurisdiction over traffic. That is the function of the California Highway Patrol. In the case of any emergency, throughout the state the telephone number to call is *911*.

Post offices

Post offices are generally open Monday to Friday from 9am to 5pm. They are usually closed on Saturdays and Sundays.

Stamps are available from vending machines in some hotels and shops, but they will cost more than from a post office. Postage rates change frequently, so always check on current tariffs. An airmail letter or postcard takes up to a week to travel from California to Europe. Parcels must be properly packaged and, if being sent by registered mail, non-removable, non-shiny tape must be used. Appropriate containers are sold at the post office. A customs declaration form must accompany any parcel being mailed abroad.

Poste Restante is known as 'General Delivery'. Letters can be addressed to any post office and must include the zip code.

Mail will only be held for 30 days, after which it will be returned to the sender, whose name and address must be on the envelope.

When collecting general delivery mail you will need some form of identification.

Postboxes are called mail boxes and are blue with 'US Mail' in white lettering.

Church in Yosemite National Park

Public transport

The majority of Californians drive cars, and outside San Francisco the public transportation system, with the exception of air travel, is not well developed. LA's metro system is being expanded, but doesn't cover many tourist areas.

By air

All the main towns in California have commercial airports. Between San Francisco (SFO) and Los Angeles (LAX) there are flights virtually every half-hour on several different airlines. Other destinations have much less frequent services. The SFO–LAX route is like a bus service, with reasonably priced tickets. Other routes are much more expensive, and it is usually better to buy tickets before arriving in the US.

Websites such as **Expedia**, **Lastminute** and, in the UK, **www.cheapflights.co.uk**, often provide the cheapest fares, though you should also check the airlines' own websites (*see pp174–5*).

By bus

Bus travel is cheap, but the distances are so great that, unless your budget is really tight, it wastes valuable time. An additional problem is that the long-distance bus stations tend to be in the less desirable parts of town. Some of the passengers on these buses can also leave a lot to be desired.

Greyhound (*www.greyhound.com*) is a major operator travelling between all the main cities. On some routes such as Los Angeles–San Francisco, Greyhound is not significantly cheaper than the cheapest air ticket. For the greatest saving buy a Discovery Pass, which is available for 7–60 days' duration. Buy tickets online at *www.discoverypass.com*.

An alternative to Greyhound is Green Tortoise, which runs weekly trips between Los Angeles and San Francisco at a very reasonable price. It caters particularly for students and younger people. See *www.greentortoise.com* or call *(800) 867 8647*.

By train
The rail system in California is not well developed. However, all major cities are connected, and Amtrak trains are clean and comfortable if not particularly fast.

USA Rail Passes are available for 15-, 30- and 45-day durations. Visit *www.amtrak.com* for details, or call *(800) 872 7245*.

Other transport
Taxis are generally quite expensive but will cost you less than a hire car.

In San Francisco, cable-car rides are a must, but these days they are as much a tourist attraction as a means of transport. Only three lines are now in operation (*see p83*).

In the San Francisco Bay area the Bay Area Rapid Transit (BART) provides a fast, efficient underground train service between San Francisco and the East Bay.

The ferries are another way to travel across the bay. The **Blue and Gold Fleet** (*tel: (415) 705 8200; www.blueandgold fleet.com*) operates between San Francisco, Sausalito, Angel Island, Tiburon, Alameda, Oakland and Vallejo. **Golden Gate Ferry** (*tel: (415) 455 2000; www.goldengateferry.org*) runs between San Francisco, Sausalito and Larkspur.

In San Diego the **San Diego Trolley** makes the 26km (16-mile) journey to the Mexican border every 15 minutes throughout the day. See *www.sdmts.com* or call *(619) 557 4555*.

Thomas Cook timetables
Details and times of long-distance bus and train services can be found in the Thomas Cook Overseas Timetable, available to buy online at *www.thomascookpublishing.com*, from Thomas Cook branches in the UK, or by calling *01733 416477*.

Senior citizens
Most hotels, motels, restaurants and museums have preferential rates for senior citizens. Usually they want to see some form of identification, but often just looking old enough will work!

Smoking
California, always a leader in social trends, has almost banned smoking. It is not allowed on public transport or in any public buildings. Smoking is not permitted in offices, or in bars and restaurants.

Smokers are generally looked upon as social pariahs and they are rapidly becoming the exception rather than the rule in California.

Sustainable tourism

Thomas Cook is a strong advocate of ethical and fairly traded tourism and believes that the travel experience should be as good for the places visited as it is for the people who visit them. That's why we firmly support The Travel Foundation, a charity that develops solutions to help improve and protect holiday destinations, their environment, traditions and culture. To find out what you can do to make a positive difference to the places you travel to and the people who live there, please visit *www.makeholidaysgreener. org.uk*

Telephones

In California telephones are everywhere. Apart from telephone kiosks there are public telephones in most bars, restaurants and hotel lobbies.

Hotels usually charge a high premium for calls from rooms. Conversely, some hotels allow local calls at no cost. Always check the rates to avoid an unpleasant surprise when checking out.

Reverse charge calls, called collect calls, can be made from any telephone by calling the operator. Dial 0 for the local operator or 00 for long-distance.

All numbers with an 800 or 877 prefix are toll-free. They can usually be

dialled from outside the US, but won't be free. At a public telephone insert a dime first (10c), which will be returned when you hang up.

For international calls dial 001, the country code and then the number (without the first 0 of the area code). A cheaper way to call internationally is to buy a prepaid phonecard, sold at many shops.

Many UK mobiles will work in the US, though call charges can be high. Contact your mobile phone company before travelling.

International codes
Australia *61*
Canada *no country code from US*
Ireland *353*
New Zealand *64*
United Kingdom *44*

Local directory information *411*
Long-distance directory enquiries (area code) +*555 1212.*

Time

California is on Pacific Standard Time, which is eight hours behind GMT. From the second Sunday in March to the first Sunday in November daylight saving time is in operation, when the clocks are put forward by one hour.

Tipping

Tips are a way of life and everyone in the service industry expects them. They are very rarely included in the bill except occasionally in restaurants when

Practical guide

The Shrine Drive-Thru Tree in Humboldt County

there is a large party. Always check. The amount is, of course, always at the discretion of the customer, but this is a general guide:

Restaurants and bars 15 to 20 per cent
Cloakroom attendants $1
Parking valet $2–3
Airport porters (skycaps) $1 per bag
Taxi drivers 15 per cent
Tour guide or driver $1 per day
Hotel porter $1 per bag
Room maid $2 per day
Hotel parking valet $2–3
Room service 15 per cent
Shoeshine 50 cents

Toilets

Public toilets, called rest rooms, are not always easy to find, but when you do they are almost always clean and free.

In cities they can be found in large department stores, bars and restaurants, and all petrol stations.

Tourist offices

Although you can write to some tourist offices to request information in advance, it makes more sense to visit the website first, as many have brochures and leaflets that can be downloaded, and can provide answers to specific questions.

California Office of Tourism *PO Box 1499, Sacramento, CA 95812. Tel: (916) 444 4429; www.visit california.com.* They can provide maps, comprehensive brochures and referrals to local Chambers of Commerce for more specific information.

Central Coast Santa Barbara Visitor Center *1 Garden St, Santa Barbara, CA 93101. Tel: (805) 965 3021. www.sbchamber.org*

Greater Los Angeles Area Los Angeles Convention and Visitors Bureau, *333 S Hope St, 18th Floor, Los Angeles, CA 90071. Tel: (213) 624 7300. www.discoverlosangeles.com*

High Sierra Lake Tahoe Visitors Authority, *3066 Lake Tahoe Blvd, South Lake Tahoe, CA 96150. Tel: (530) 544 5050. www.tahoesouth.com.*

North Coast North Coast Tourism Council, *1034 2nd St, Eureka, CA 95501. Tel: (800) 346 3482. www.northcoastca.com*

Orange County Anaheim Visitor and Convention Bureau, *800 W Katella Ave, Anaheim, CA 92802. Tel: (714) 765 8888. www.anaheimoc.org*

Palm Springs Area Palm Springs Visitors Center, *2901 N Palm Canyon Dr, Palm Springs, CA 92262. Tel: (800) 347 7746. www.visitpalmsprings.com*

Palm Springs Desert Resorts Communities Convention and Visitors Authority, *70–100 Hwy 111, Rancho Mirage, CA 92270. Tel: (800) 967 3767. www.palmspringsusa.com*

San Diego International Visitor Information Center, *1040 1/3 W Broadway, San Diego, CA 92101. Tel: (619) 236 1212. www.sandiego.org*

San Francisco Bay Area Visitor Information Center, *900 Market St, San Francisco, CA 94102. Tel: (415) 391 2000. www.onlyinsanfrancisco.com*

Travellers with disabilities

California is more responsive to the needs of disabled people than many places.

At airports there are always good facilities including special lifts (elevators), toilets and availability of wheelchairs.

Most hotels, public buildings and museums now have wheelchair access and toilet facilities. Any public building erected or renovated since 1982 is required by law to have extensive facilities for the disabled, including access and toilets. It is always a good idea to check with your destination to verify that adequate facilities are available.

Disabled parking areas are widely available and hefty fines are given for illegal use of these spaces. They are always marked in blue and with a wheelchair symbol. You need a relevant permit/sticker to park here. Throughout the state people will be sympathetic to the problems of travellers with disabilities and generally very helpful.

What to take

Most people find that they take too much to California. You can find everything you can get at home and more, and it is generally cheaper. Clothes are particularly good value. The best advice is to leave plenty of room in your suitcase for the many bargains that you will inevitably want to take home with you.

Index

192

Acknowledgements

Thomas Cook Publishing wishes to thank the photographers, picture libraries and other organisations, to whom the copyright belongs, for the photographs in this book.

ALAMY 1, 93
KAREN BEAULAH 157
BEN GLICKMAN 15
DREAMSTIME (tangducminh) 83, (photoquest) 87, (Mark Rasmussen) 94 & 115, (John Turner) 143
MARY EVANS PICTURE LIBRARY 30
FRED GEBHART AND MAXINE CASS 13, 19, 22, 28, 31, 32, 38, 39, 41, 42, 44, 51, 53, 55, 56, 60, 63, 66, 67, 69, 71, 73, 77, 92, 100, 103, 105, 106, 109, 111, 113, 118, 120, 123, 127, 128, 129, 133, 135, 136, 139, 144, 145, 167
ROBERT HOLMES 20, 23
LESLEY McCAVE 74, 146, 150, 179
WIKIMEDIA COMMONS 97 (Infratec), 158 (GreatInca), 173 (Minnaert), 185 (David Maximillian Waterman), 188 (Jan Kronsell)
LISA VOORMEIJ 5, 80, 119, 141
WORLD PICTURES/PHOTOSHOT 16, 17, 21, 25, 29, 35, 43, 47, 57, 65, 99, 101, 125

The remaining pictures are held in the AA PHOTO LIBRARY and were taken by BARRIE SMITH with the exception of page 107 which was taken by HAROLD HARRIS and page 161 which was taken by PETER WILSON.

For CAMBRIDGE PUBLISHING MANAGEMENT LIMITED:
Project editor: Thomas Willsher
Typesetter: Donna Pedley
Proofreaders: Ceinwen Sinclair & Jan McCann
Indexer: Marie Lorimer

SEND YOUR THOUGHTS TO
BOOKS@THOMASCOOK.COM

We're committed to providing the very best up-to-date information in our travel guides and constantly strive to make them as useful as they can be. You can help us to improve future editions by letting us have your feedback. If you've made a wonderful discovery on your travels that we don't already feature, if you'd like to inform us about recent changes to anything that we do include, or if you simply want to let us know your thoughts about this guidebook and how we can make it even better – we'd love to hear from you.

Send us ideas, discoveries and recommendations today and then look out for your valuable input in the next edition of this title.

Emails to the above address, or letters to the traveller guides Series Editor, Thomas Cook Publishing, PO Box 227, Coningsby Road, Peterborough PE3 8SB, UK.

Please don't forget to let us know which title your feedback refers to!